# GET STARTED *in* FINGER KNITTING

# GET STARTED *in* FINGER KNITTING

PATTERNS *and* INSTRUCTIONS *for* MAKING CHUNKY BLANKETS, COZY PILLOWS, *and* CUTE STUFFIES *by* HAND

SABRINA-ROSE BENEDICT

BETTER DAY BOOKS®
HAPPY • CREATIVE • CURATED

*Get Started in Finger Knitting* © 2025 by Sabrina-Rose Benedict and Better Day Books, an imprint of Schiffer Publishing, Ltd.

Publisher: Peg Couch
Cover and Book Designer: Lindsay Hess
Production Designer: Llara Pazdan
Project Stylist: Lori Wenger
Project Photographer: Jason Masters
Step Photographer: Sabrina-Rose Benedict
Editor: Colleen Dorsey
Assistant Editor: Jules Hostetter



Library of Congress Control Number: 2025930726

ISBN: 978-0-7643-7004-5
ePub: 978-1-5073-0630-7
Printed in China
10 9 8 7 6 5 4 3

Published by Better Day Books, an imprint of Schiffer Publishing, Ltd.

MIX
Paper | Supporting responsible forestry
FSC® C167893

BETTER DAY BOOKS®

SCHIFFER PUBLISHING

**Better Day Books**
Email: hello@betterdaybooks.com
Web: www.betterdaybooks.com
Visit us on Instagram!
@better_day_books

**Schiffer Publishing**
4880 Lower Valley Road
Atglen, PA 19310
Phone: 610-593-1777
Fax: 610-593-2002
Email: info@schifferbooks.com
Web: www.schifferbooks.com

# DEDICATION

To my husband, whose endless love and encouragement sustain me.

To my children, who are my constant motivation and remind me why I keep going.

And to my parents and siblings, each of whom has supported me in meaningful ways throughout my business journey.

98

58

52

92

136

102

# CONTENTS

# WELCOME!

If you want to embark on a new beginner-friendly hobby, you have come to the right place! Many people think of knitting as done only with needles or by a machine, but did you know there is another way of knitting? You can toss those knitting needles right out the door, because this book will teach you how to knit with just your fingers! I am so glad you are here and ready to learn.

Several years ago, I was in search of a new hobby. I came across a chunky-knit blanket, and I was determined to learn how to finger-knit one for myself. From the moment I made my first blanket, I decided that finger knitting was something I was going to master. My first knit blanket was far from perfect, but I was ecstatic that I had learned something new. I wanted to further my crafting abilities, so I learned traditional knitting with needles and even a little bit of crochet, but the craft of finger knitting was what stuck with me. With a lot of practice, I finally mastered making chunky-knit blankets and began finger-knitting stuffies.

My hobby quickly developed into a small business of making and selling my finger-knit products. Soon after launching my business, I noticed that many followers were interested in learning how to make the products I was selling. This sparked the idea of teaching others how to finger-knit and spreading my joy of learning. Going from a behind-the-scenes creator to being in the spotlight teaching others how to finger-knit was an intimidating process at first, but taking that leap of faith was entirely worth it. Teaching others became my passion and brought a new purpose to my business.

Finger knitting has quickly become a popular hobby that people of all ages are eager to learn, and this ultimate beginner guide to the craft is my latest way of reaching out to more potential finger-knitting enthusiasts! This book includes foundational projects like the Blanket, beginner-friendly patterns to build your skills, and a few intermediate patterns to challenge you. You can make all the projects to enjoy yourself or to gift to others.

It's time to start warming up those fingers and getting ready to learn a new skill that is quick to pick up and so enjoyable! I hope you fall in love with the craft just like I did. Happy knitting!

Sam-Rose Benedict

# MEET SABRINA-ROSE

We sat down with Sabrina-Rose to learn a little more about her and her finger-knitting journey. Join us!

**How did you get into finger knitting? Were you always crafty?**
Growing up, I never really thought of myself as a crafty person, but, looking back, I was always drawn to art and DIY projects. I loved drawing, braiding hair, playing with makeup, anything creative. So, I guess I've always had a crafty side, after all. I first discovered finger knitting through a YouTube video on how to make a chunky-knit blanket, and I've been hooked ever since!

**You have cultivated an enormous following of more than 800,000 people online. How did that happen?**
In August 2022, I posted a reel of myself making a chunky-knit blanket on Instagram, and it went viral, gaining over six million views. That one video took my account from under 1,000 followers to over 80,000 in just a few weeks. Once I figured out the type of content that really connected with people, I kept going. Since then, those videos have helped me grow to more than 800,000 followers on Instagram and over 1.6 million across all my social platforms.

**Why do you think people are so drawn to finger knitting?**
I think people are drawn to finger knitting because it looks relaxing and approachable. It's a simple, hands-on craft that people of all ages can learn quickly and genuinely enjoy. The chunky-knit blanket, in particular, really grabs attention because it looks doable for beginners to learn, and the end result is something cozy and beautiful.

**What do you love about finger knitting?**
The creativity it allows! When I first started, I was drawn to how relaxing it felt, and I loved being able to sell the chunky blankets I made. But once I started experimenting with making stuffies, it opened up a whole new world. I really enjoy the challenge of creating new designs and getting to pour my creativity into each pattern.

**How do you incorporate so much expression and creativity into your patterns?**
A lot of it comes down to practice. When I first started making stuffies, I honestly had no idea what I was doing—I just experimented like crazy. I came up with all kinds of "techniques" that probably wouldn't make sense to anyone else if I tried to explain them (and I've had to keep adjusting those methods over time to make them teachable!). But I was determined to make each stuffie look the way I imagined, no matter what. As I kept learning and refining my skills, it became easier to bring more expression and creativity into each design.

**What are some of the benefits of finger knitting?**
One of my favorite things about finger knitting is that it gives you something to be proud of and a real sense of accomplishment. Beyond that, it's incredibly relaxing and great for stress relief. That's actually why I included my Stress-Ball Buddy pattern in this book! You get to unwind while making it, and then you have a cute little stress ball to help with future stress too.

**In addition to being the master of finger knitting, you are also a busy mama with two little ones. How do you manage it all?**
If I'm being honest, I'm still figuring out how to manage it all and find balance. Most days, it's not easy, but my family always comes first. There are plenty of times I've had to shift my business plans to focus on what my little ones need in the moment. I'm really lucky to have my husband's support; he's amazing at picking up where I leave off, especially with household stuff. I definitely couldn't "manage it all" without him!

**What other creative pursuits do you enjoy?**
I've always loved cooking and baking! With two little ones and my business, it can be a bit more stressful now than it used to be, but I'm hopeful that one day I'll find my way back to it as a creative outlet. Lately, I've also been really enjoying gardening during the spring and summer.

**Other than this book, what's exciting in your life right now?**
Anything new I'm working on is always exciting! Whether it's designing a fresh pattern or creating new DIY finger-knitting kits, I love the process. Recently, I've been working on a Jellyfish kit and a Christmas tree kit that I'm really excited about!

**What are your favorite yarn colors?**
I'm all about bright-colored variegated yarn! I tend to stick to neutral-colored clothing because I'm not one to stand out, but, for some reason, when it comes to my stuffies, I just love the bold, vibrant colors. It adds so much personality to each one!

**What does a perfect day look like for you?**
A perfect day for me would be filled with lots of laughter from my kids, good food, a little show to watch, and, of course, plenty of knitting!

**What's your favorite beverage and music to enjoy while you're finger knitting?**
Boba tea! Or anything sweet and fruity. I don't usually listen to music while I'm knitting—I prefer watching a movie or show. But when I'm packing orders, I love to listen to hymns.

**What do you hope readers will get from this book? And from finger knitting?**
I hope readers will discover (or rediscover) a love and passion for knitting through this book. Maybe they've tried traditional knitting or crochet in the past, and it just didn't stick. My goal is for this book to show them how relaxing and enjoyable finger knitting can be, and for it to become a craft they truly connect with.

**Where can we connect with you and join your crafty community?**
Instagram is my main platform where I connect with other finger knitters and share in the creativity of the community. I love seeing all the amazing creations people make and building relationships with others who share the same passion!

**SABRINA-ROSE BENEDICT** rocketed to internet fame after her finger-knitted blankets and pillows charmed followers around the world. Now, her not-so-small business, Sab's Stuffies, carries blankets, pillows, animal stuffies of all sizes, and a collection of DIY kits on everything from ghosts to snowmen. Find out more about her at www.sabsstuffies.com.

# GETTING STARTED

Finger knitting is a skill that uses a limited amount of tools and materials and that is largely based on a set of essential techniques that can create a ton of variety. In this Getting Started section, we'll go over all the details a total beginner needs to know to set you up for success!

# TOOLS AND MATERIALS

Let's discuss the tools and materials needed for the projects within this book. Here's the good news, and it's one of my favorite parts about this craft: There is not a lot involved, as far as tools and materials go, to be able to finger-knit and make stunning creations!

## *Yarn*

The most important material you need for finger knitting is yarn, and lots of it. The yarn used in my finger-knit creations has been called many different things, such as chunky or big blanket yarn, chunky chenille yarn, jumbo yarn, and more. There are various brands of yarn, and each brand and store may use different names for this kind of yarn. Once you understand what you're looking for, though, you can easily determine if the product you're examining is correct or not for your needs. What you're looking for in finger knitting is yarn that is extra thick and bulky, typically 100% polyester, with a yarn weight of jumbo size 7. When picking out yarn for your projects, refer to the label to check these details—or the listing description if you're shopping online.

The sizes of each skein of yarn will vary depending on the brand or store the yarn is bought from. Typically, a skein contains from 28 to 32 yards (25–29 m) of yarn, but some giant skeins contain up to 72 yards (65 m) each! The amount of yarn needed for any particular project will vary. In this book, each individual pattern will specify the amount of yarn needed for it.

There is a wide variety of color options to choose from out there. Solid-color yarn (dark, light, neon, neutral, etc.), variegated yarn with two or more colors, and even tie-dye yarn all are options when picking yarn for your patterns. Choosing colors for blankets and stuffies is one of the most exciting parts of creating a new project! I love how customizable a project can be just by switching to a different color.

The exact yarns you will be able to purchase will vary depending on where you live and what stores and brands are nearby. Here in the US, my favorite places to shop for yarn are Hobby Lobby (where I buy Yarn Bee Eternal Bliss), Michaels (where I buy Bernat Blanket Big), and Yarnspirations.com (where I buy Bernat Blanket Extra Thick).

## *Alternative Yarns*

While I personally have only ever used chunky chenille-type yarn for my projects, there are a few other yarn types that are big enough to be used in finger knitting.

My friend Jessica of Stay Cozy Creative Co. is the queen of all things tube yarn! She creates beautiful knit projects using big tube yarn. On the outside, the yarn is cotton, but on the inside, it's filled with "soft, pillow-like polyester fibers." It's not a perfect alternative to chunky chenille yarn—specifically, it doesn't work great for my stuffie patterns—but it is perfect for blankets!

If you are searching for an eco-friendly and natural alternative, I recommend looking into chunky merino wool. I do not know much about merino wool, and I have never personally used it in my finger-knitting work, but I know it is 100% wool and can be used for these projects. Just be aware that it can shed quite a bit!

## *Fiberfill*

To stuff your stuffies, you will need some fiberfill (sometimes known by the brand name Poly-Fil). You can find this at any of your local craft stores or online. Each brand will have a slightly different feel, and some are softer than others, but they will all get the job done. The fiberfill will be featured only on the inside of the stuffies. My personal favorite brand to use is Fairfield Poly-Fil Premium Fiber. The amount of fiberfill needed will vary from project to project; at the start of each project in this book, I'll indicate how much you will need for that project.

## *Scissors*

The only tool you truly need in order to finger-knit is a pair of scissors. Being able to cut the yarn is an essential part of making any blankets or stuffie. I recommend a good pair of sharp fabric scissors. Any scissors will do the job, but sharp scissors will cut the yarn the best for your finger-knit creations!

## *Measuring Tape or Ruler*

A tape measure or ruler can be useful for beginners. It's easy to accidentally overestimate or underestimate the sizes of your loops and yarn lengths, which can sometimes throw off your finished result. Once you get the hang of finger knitting, though, you likely won't need to use a measuring tool anymore.

## *Lighter*

A lighter is not an essential tool to make these patterns, but in the following Basic Techniques section, I will explain how you can use a lighter to attach two different pieces or colors of yarn. The lighter method is an alternative to the knot method, though, so you can use the knot method instead if you don't have or don't want to use a lighter.

# BASIC TECHNIQUES

Don't skip this section! You will want to review the basic techniques presented here and try at least some of them out before you dive into the projects. Refer back to this section as needed as you make each project!

## Making a Slip Knot

Every finger-knit project begins with a basic slip knot. This slip knot serves as the start of the foundation chain, or what I call the chain row / first row.

1 **Find your starting point.** Start by leaving a tail yarn of about 8" (20 cm) long. That is, you'll start your slip knot 8" (20 cm) up from the start of the yarn piece.

2 **Pick up a section.** Grab the yarn with your right and left hand, with around 4" (10 cm) of yarn in between them. The tail should be to the left.

3 **Cross the yarn.** With your right hand, bring the yarn to your left hand so the yarn is crossed over and you have created a loop.

4 **Insert your fingers.** Insert your left thumb and index finger into the loop you just created. I like to hold my tail yarn in the palm of my hand with my pinky and ring finger so it's out of the way.

5 **Grab the yarn.** With your left thumb and index finger, grab the working yarn (from your right hand) and pull a little bit of it through the loop. This will create another loop.

6 **Tighten the slip knot.** Keeping ahold of the new loop you just created, pull down on your tail yarn to tighten the slip knot.

7 **Adjust the size.** Slip knots for stuffies should be about 1" (2.5 cm) wide; for blankets, they should be about 2½" (6.4 cm) wide. If you need to make the loop of your slip knot smaller, hold it at the knot and pull down on your working yarn (shown here). If you need to make the loop of your slip knot bigger, hold it at the knot and pull up on the loop on the side that your working yarn is on.

## Foundational Chain Row

The chain row is the foundation that any finger-knit project is worked on, which is why it's also referred to as the foundation row. After making a slip knot, you will continue pulling up loops with your working yarn until you have the correct amount of loops "chained on," which completes your chain row. I consider the chain row to be Row 1 for my patterns, and the row after that to be Row 2. But many pattern creators write their patterns with the chain row as its own element and call the row after it Row 1. Everyone will have different preferences and methods of keeping track of rows—just make sure you understand what the writer of the pattern you're following means!

1 **Insert your fingers.** After making a slip knot (which counts as loop 1), start to make loop 2 by putting your left thumb and pointer finger into the loop of the slip knot . . .

2 **Grab a loop.** . . . grabbing and pulling up another loop of the working yarn . . .

3 **Straighten.** . . . and straightening it out. Make sure the new loop is the same size as the slip knot.

4 **Continue pulling loops through.** Continue this pattern of pulling up a new loop through the previous loop until you have the total number of loops chained on that you need (including the slip-knot loop in the count). Make sure that each of the loops is the same size, referring to the size needed for the specific pattern you are working on.

## Basic Knit Stitch

All the projects in this book will also require the use of a basic knit stitch. A knit stitch is simply pulling up a loop of the working yarn from the backside of the project, bringing it to the front side. The loop from the row below will rest behind the new loop pulled up. The knit stitch creates a "V"-shaped look. Some makers prefer to use a "pulling up" method, while others prefer a "pushing up" method. I prefer the "pulling up" method because it helps me pull up my next loop as close as possible to the previous loop, ensuring that I have a tightly knit project. Choose whichever method you feel comfortable with.

### *Method 1: Pulling Up Loops*

1 **Insert your finger in the next loop available.** Put your left index finger through the loop from the front of the project and grab on to the working yarn (which is at the back of the project).

2 **Pull up the loop.** Pull a loop of the working yarn through to the front of the project.

### *Method 2: Pushing Up Loops*

1 **Make a loop.** Grab the working yarn (which is at the back of the project) with your right hand and make a loop with it.

2 **Push the loop through.** Push the loop of working yarn through to the front of the project.

## Fixing a Slipped Loop

A slipped loop (commonly known as a dropped stitch in regular knitting) is when one of your loops falls (or slips) out, leaving you with a loose loop from the previous row. You'll usually catch this while checking your work. A skipped loop, in contrast, is when you accidentally forget a loop in a row. You'll typically catch this when you count your row back and realize that there are fewer loops than you started with. Fixing a skipped loop is more of a challenge than fixing a slipped loop—your best bet will be to undo your work all the way back to the skipped loop. (Make it a habit to count your stitches for each row as you go, so that you never have to undo too much work!) Below is the method for how to fix a slipped loop.

1 **Find the correct column.** From your slipped loop, follow the column straight away, perpendicular to the slipped loop, until you reach your current working row's loop in the same column. This is the loop you'll start adjusting with.

2 **Manually unpick the column.** Flip your work over. Slip the loop out, then continue slipping the loops in that column out all the way down to your original slipped loop.

3 **Fix the first slipped loop.** Pull the original slipped loop through to the front side, insert your left finger into the last loop you manually slipped out, and pull that loop over and up through the slipped loop.

4 **Fix the rest of the column.** Repeat all the way back up the column. In this photo, I have finished fixing the entire column.

## Attaching Two Skeins of Yarn

When it comes time to attach a new skein of yarn or change the color you are working with, there are two options: the knot method and the lighter method. The knot method will work well for all of the projects in this book, but let's learn both so you have a choice for future projects.

### *Knot Method*

The knot method is exactly what it sounds like and is straightforward and beginner-friendly. One of its downsides, though, is that it can be visible within your work, particularly in a blanket. I like to use this method for all my stuffie patterns, where I can easily hide the knot inside the project.

1 **Make the knot.** Take the end of the working yarn of your project and the end of the new piece of yarn you want to attach to it. Tie them together directly behind the last loop made with a double knot, nice and tight.

2 **Trim the excess.** Cut the excess yarn off the knot so you are left with just a small, low-profile knot.

## Attaching Two Skeins of Yarn *(continued)*

### *Lighter Method*

The lighter or burning method is another great way to attach two pieces of yarn. It gives a more seamless look without any extra bumps. However, it's not as beginner-friendly and may take some practice to get right. If you get a good connection, this method is a sure way to guarantee your attached yarn pieces are secure.

Note: If you try this method, do so carefully, since you are working with a fire. Do not do this on a flammable surface. Give the burnt pieces a few seconds to cool slightly before touching them to roll them out.

1 **Light the ends.** Take the very end of each piece of yarn you want to join. Using a lighter, burn the core (the little hard piece of plastic at the center of the yarn) of both pieces.

2 **Join the ends.** Stick the lit ends together firmly.

3 **Roll the join.** Depending on how the two ends burn and attach, there could be a hard piece at the join, so it is important to roll out the burnt join with your fingers once they are attached.

4 **Test the join.** It's crucial to test the yarn once attached, to make sure you have a good connection. Pull firmly on each end of the yarn.

## Making a Circle and Row 2

When making something "in the round" (a project that is not flat but, rather, circular, like many of the projects in this book), you will need to transform your chain row (Row 1) into a circle before continuing.

Once you get past the steps of creating the circle and adding the second row, it will become easier. It might take some time and practice to get it down, but practice makes perfect!

1 **Form the circle.** Take the tail yarn of your chain row and push it through the very last loop that you made for the chain.

2 **Adjust the circle.** Pull the tail yarn through until the knot from the slip knot is right at the loop that the tail yarn has been pulled through.

3 **Find the correct loop.** Make sure the tail yarn and working yarn are pointing away from you, then find the correct top loop to the right side. This is not the loop that your last loop from the chain was pulled through, but the one right after that. I'm pointing to it here.

4 **Pull up a loop.** Pull your working yarn through this top loop to make another loop.

## Making a Circle and Row 2 *(continued)*

**5 Pull up more loops.** Continue pulling up loops through each of the top loops, one at a time. Here, I've pulled through 3 more loops.

**6 Keep working your way around.** Keep going. You will notice that the chain row will flip inside out as you go around the row. Stop right when you reach the second-to-last loop (read on to the next step).

**7 Skip the slip knot.** As you continue, make sure to skip over the actual knot from the slip knot—you do not want to try to force a loop through that knot!

**8 Move the tail yarn.** At this point the tail yarn has worked itself to the top of your work and is getting in your way. Push the tail yarn back through the center of the piece, so it is down and out of the way.

**9 Pull up the second-to-last loop.** The second-to-last loop will be where the tail yarn is inserted through. Pull up another loop through that loop as usual.

**10 Find the last loop.** The last loop that you will pull a new loop through to complete the row will be pointing vertically.

**11 Insert your finger.** Insert your finger into this last loop and twist it slightly so the loop is facing the same direction as the rest of the loops.

**12 Complete the last loop of the row.** Grab the working yarn with your finger and pull up the last loop of the second row as normal. You've completed Row 2!

## Increasing

Not all projects will include increasing, but it's an important step to know for the patterns that do. Increasing is quite simple. All you need to do is pull up a loop in between the previous loop made and the next loop to be made. Then you'll continue knitting like normal (or at least until the next time the pattern says to increase!).

1 **Find your increase spot.** Instead of pulling up a new loop through the next loop in the row, like we did in the basic knit stitch, find the horizontal, lower loop from the previous completed row that sits in between the regular loop you just pulled up and the next loop you would normally pull another loop through. I have my finger through it in this picture (and am working toward the right)

2 **Pull up the increase loop.** Pull up a new loop of your working yarn through this loop from the previous row. The new loop you just created should sit in between your last regular loop of your current row and the next loop you're about to do in your current row. I'm pointing to the new increase loop just made in this picture.

## Decreasing

Decreasing can be a little more challenging than increasing, mainly because different creators have different ways of decreasing. Here's how you will decrease when reading and working with the patterns in this book. To decrease, instead of pulling up a new loop with the working yarn in the next loop over as normal, you will instead pull that next loop **over the top of and down around** the previous loop made. Then you will continue knitting like normal (or at least until the next time the pattern says to decrease!).

1 **Insert your finger.** Put your left finger through the next loop over (I'm working toward the right here), but, this time, don't grab the working yarn like you normally would.

2 **Grab the previous loop.** With your right hand, grab the previous loop made in the row.

3 **Decrease.** Put the loop your left index finger is through over the top of and down around the previous loop.

## Counting Rows "In the Round"

When making a project "in the round," counting rows will look the same as when counting rows for a flat blanket, but you'll need to know how to find where a row ends. When you are working on a row and find yourself working the loop that is lined up with the tail yarn, that is how you know you have to continue one more loop over in order to complete the full row. Once you complete a row, you can count down the column of rows to see how many rows you have completed. Once you get past the second row, this is how you can easily keep track of your rows.

# Closing a Project

The finishing method is slightly different for each end of a project—the tail-yarn end or the working-yarn end. The tail-yarn end is at the bottom of the stuffie where the loops are closed; these can also be called the bottom loops. The working-yarn end will have open loops, where you just completed your last row; these can also be referred to as top loops.

## *At the Tail Yarn*

To close up a circle on the side of the tail yarn (which is typically at the bottom of a stuffie, after the item has been stuffed), you will be working to the right. It's important to work to the right, not to the left, for best security.

1 **Insert the tail yarn through the next bottom loop.** Start from the outside of the project. Grab the tail yarn and insert it through the bottom loop one over to the right from it, then gently tighten the yarn. This is similar to an overhand stitch.

2 **Continue around.** Next insert it through the next bottom loop over and gently tighten again. Continue this pattern until you get to the last bottom loop, making sure you are tightening each loop as you go.

3 **Knot to finish.** Once you've tightened all around the circle and completely closed up the hole of the circle, make a double knot at the base of the tail yarn, snugged up neatly against the bottom of the project. Then push the remaining tail yarn and its double knot up through the center of the hole you just closed up, so the strand of yarn and the knot are now entirely on the inside of the project.

## Closing a Project *(continued)*

### *At the Working Yarn*

Closing the working-yarn end is very similar to closing the tail-yarn end.

**1 Insert the working yarn through the next loop.** Once the last row of knitting is finished, cut the working yarn to leave yourself about 8" (20 cm) loose. Working to the left, take this 8" (20 cm) length of working yarn and insert it through the next loop, starting from the inside of the project and toward the outside.

**2 Continue around.** Go through a few more loops and then tighten the weave, making sure to have your thumb inserted through the last loop of the row to prevent the loops from slipping out as you pull to tighten. Continue this pattern through to the last loop.

**3 Knot to finish.** Once you've completely closed up the circle, make a double knot at the base of the working yarn, snugged up neatly against the project. Then push the remaining working yarn and its double knot up through the center of the hole you just closed up, so the strand of yarn and the knot are now entirely on the inside of the project.

For some bonus finger-knitting tutorials and more finger-knitting fun, check out my YouTube channel! www.youtube.com/@sabsstuffies

# PROJECTS

You've collected your yarn, reviewed the basic techniques, and are ready to dive into a project! The projects in this book build upon one another, but that doesn't necessarily mean you can't skip around a little bit. Start by making the Blanket so that you can get the hang of the craft.

***Finished Size:***
48" × 35" (121 × 89 cm)

***Skill Level:***
Beginner

# BLANKET

In 2019, I picked up some chunky yarn from my local craft store and created my first chunky-knit blanket. There were not a lot of detailed resources available at the time, so it took a lot of perseverance and trial and error to complete. Although the finished blanket was nowhere near perfect, it sparked my passion for designing the products I make today! The classic chunky-knit blanket will forever hold a special place in my heart because it reminds me of where I started, so it was an easy choice to make it the first project in this book.

A blanket is the ultimate beginner-friendly and foundational project to teach you several basic techniques for finger knitting that will be utilized in various other finger-knit projects throughout this book. This pattern will teach you how to make a small throw blanket. I have also added some tips and tricks for how to make a larger blanket.

## SUPPLIES

**Chunky blanket yarn:**
Light gray: 56 yards (51.2 m) (two 28-yard / 25.6 m skeins)
Taupe: 56 yards (51.2 m) (two 28-yard / 25.6 m skeins)
Ivory: 56 yards (51.2 m) (two 28-yard / 25.6 m skeins)

**Scissors**

**Lighter (optional)**

All finished sizes, yarn lengths, and fiberfill quantities are approximate.

## CHAIN ROW (ROW 1)

**1 Make a slip knot.** With your first color (light gray), create a slip knot that has an 8" (20 cm) tail. Make the slip-knot loop about 2½" (6.4 cm) or three fingers wide. Remember, the slip knot counts as loop 1 of your chain row!

**TIP:** Your tail yarn should stay on the left side if you are working from left to right for your chain row. If you prefer to work in the opposite direction (right to left) to start, your tail should stay on the right side.

**2 Make the chain row.** Make the chain row by pulling up loops, each around 2½" (6.4 cm) or three fingers wide for this first row, until you have a total of 25 loops in your chain (including the slip-knot loop). The loops in your chain row will be bigger than the loops in the following rows—this will prevent the edges of your blanket from curving in and will help your blanket to stay straight.

## ROW 2

**3 Find the starting point for Row 2.** Find the loop in the middle of the chain row that is one over to the left of the last loop made.

**4 Prepare to start Row 2.** Insert your thumb or finger as a guide, putting it through that center loop where the next loop needs to be pulled up through.

**5 Pull up a loop.** Pull the working yarn through the center loop to create a new loop. Make this loop (and all following loops in the row except the last) smaller than you made the loops in Row 1—they should now be around two tight fingers or 1" (2.5 cm) wide. (If you prefer to make a looser-knit blanket, you can make your loops bigger.)

**6 Check your count.** This new loop that you've just pulled through is loop 2 of the second row (Row 2). The last loop of the chain (first) row becomes loop 1 of Row 2.

**7 Continue the row.** Continue pulling up loops through the center loops of the chain, one after the other, working your way left.

**8 Finish the row.** Make the last loop of the row slightly bigger, around 2" (5 cm) wide. Once the last loop (loop 25) is pulled up, Row 2 is complete. Remember, this is loop 25, but you pulled up only 24 loops for Row 2, due to skipping the first loop—that last loop of the first row became loop 1 of Row 2.

**REMEMBER:** When making a blanket, the last loop in every row (on both sides) should always be slightly bigger than the rest of the loops in the row.

**TIP:** When you complete every row, you should always have the same number of total loops across that you chained on in the first row—in this case, 25. Missing a loop can be common when making a chunky-knit blanket. To prevent this, count your loops as you go or count your loops back after you finish a row.

## REMAINING NORMAL ROWS

**9 Start Row 3.** To start a new row, skip the last loop added in the previous row and pull up a new loop through the second loop over, just like you did when starting Row 2.

**10 Continue Row 3.** Continue pulling up consistently sized loops down the row.

**11 Finish Row 3.** Pull up the last loop of the row, making it slightly bigger than the rest of the loops in the row, as usual. You'll always end a row by pulling up a loop through the last loop of the row!

**12 Continue until you have 22 rows.** Now start a new row again by skipping the last loop and pulling up a new loop from the second loop over. You'll always start a new row this way. Continue making rows until you have completed 22 total rows (including the chain row) with your initial color (light gray). See step 16 for more guidance on counting rows.

## CHANGING TO A NEW SKEIN

**13 Prepare to change skeins.** When changing to a new color in the blanket, do it at the end of a row before pulling up the larger last loop—your new color will be the last loop of the row instead. (If you are adding a new skein of yarn that is the same color as the previous skein, you can add it anywhere within a row—it doesn't have to be at the end of a row.)

**14 Join the yarn ends.** Tie a double knot or use the lighter method to attach the two pieces of yarn. I'll be tying for this tutorial. Cut the excess yarn on either side of the knot, but not too closely, in case the knot loosens or slips over time.

**TIP:** For any of the colors in this blanket, it's okay if you use up your two skeins of that color but have not necessarily completed 22 rows, since everyone's loops will vary in size.

**15 Finish Row 22 and continue.** Pull up the last loop of the row, now using the new color. Then continue knitting and pulling up new loops like normal. Knit 22 total rows of your middle color (taupe), change to your final color (ivory), and knit 21 total rows of that color—but, see page 42 for how to check your work as you go. We will pick up in 17 for to learn how to knit the last, closing row of your final color (Row 22 of that color).

## COUNTING ROWS AND MEASURING

16 **Check your work as you go.** While this is not necessary for a solid-color blanket, it is useful for multicolor blankets. It will help you ensure that all your colored sections are evenly spaced. You can choose between the two methods presented here.

**METHOD #1: COUNTING ROWS:** Count down the number of rows you have for your first color or section. If you are having trouble seeing the separation of rows as you count the loops down, pull on the loops slightly to see the separation better. Every blanket will have a different number of rows per color, depending on the number of loops chained on, the loops' sizes, the color pattern, etc. Once you count how many rows the first section of color has, ensure that the next section of color has the same number of rows.

**METHOD #2: MEASURING TAPE:** Once the first section of color is complete, take a measuring tape and measure the length of that first color section. As you move on to the next section of color, continue to measure its length as you work. Knit until you reach the same length as your last section.

## FINISHING

17 **Finish the next-to-last row.** Pull up your last loop in Row 21 of the third color like normal.

18 **Start the finishing row.** Pull up your first loop of the new row (Row 22 of the third color) as usual. With this loop and as you proceed for the entire finishing row, make the loops bigger, like the first row of loops: about 2½" (6.4 cm) or three fingers wide.

**19** **Get ready to close off a loop.** As usual, the last loop of the previous row is now loop 1 of the current row. So, now that there are 2 loops pulled up in this current row, insert the index finger and thumb of your right hand through loop 1 . . .

**20** **Close off the loop.** . . . to grab loop 2 and pull it up through loop 1, so that loop 1 goes over the top of and down around to the base of loop 2. In simpler words, take loop 1 and pull it down over loop 2. (Note: In the photos for steps 19 and 20, I am working toward the left for my last row on this blanket, so I am inserting my right hand through loop 1. If I was working the opposite way, I would use my left hand.)

**21** **Stop to check.** This will leave you with just 1 loop, which is the last loop you made in the row, loop 2.

**22** **Repeat to make and close off a new loop.** As usual, pull up loop 3 in the next loop over. Then, repeat steps 19–20 to pull loop 2 over the top of and down around loop 3.

**23** **Continue this way down the row.** Repeat these steps all the way down the row until there is just 1 loop left and nowhere to go with it. That is, pull up loop 4 and pull loop 3 over loop 4, then pull up loop 5 and pull loop 5 over loop 4, etc.

**24** **Trim the yarn.** Cut the working yarn off the skein, leaving a tail of about 8" (20 cm) of working yarn.

**25** **Make a very basic knot.** Pull the working yarn through the last loop and tighten it to close off the last loop. Be careful not to pull your working yarn too hard, or it may snap.

**TIP:** Ensure that you have enough yarn (about four or five times the width of your blanket) on your last skein left to close off the blanket. If you don't have enough, undo your last row and close off there, or attach a new skein of yarn when you run out.

**26 Get ready to weave in the end.** Going in the opposite direction from the direction the final row was worked—so, back toward the right, in this case—find the last loop of the row. I've inserted my finger through both strands of it here.

**27 Weave through one loop.** Pull the excess working yarn through both strands of this loop, weaving it in and out a few times.

**28 Make a new knot.** Now go one row down and pull the excess working yarn through, creating a loop, and then pull the yarn back through that same loop to create a knot.

**29 Make the final cut.** Gently pull the yarn to tighten the knot. Then cut the excess yarn at the base of the knot and push the knot under the row. Repeat steps 26–29 for the tail yarn on the other end of the blanket.

***Finished Size:***
18" × 8" (46 × 20 cm)

***Skill Level:***
Beginner

# LONG PILLOW POUF

My mom and dad have supported my creative endeavors since my finger-knitting journey started. For as long as I can remember, my dad has always had a favorite spot on the couch, and, a few years ago, I gifted him one of the first long pillow poufs I ever made. That pillow pouf has now become a part of his spot on the couch! Every time I am home over the holidays and summer months, I see him using his pillow pouf, and it brings me happiness to know how much he uses it.

The patterns for pillow poufs were the first projects that I created outside of blankets, and they are how I learned to knit "in the round." It was a little challenging to adapt to this form of finger knitting, but it also led me to explore creating my first chunky-knit stuffie, Ollie the Octopus, which also features in this book. Now, fluff up your pillows and let the knitting begin!

## SUPPLIES

**Chunky blanket yarn:**
Color of choice: 30 yards (27.4 m)

**Fiberfill: 11 ounces (310 g)**

**Scissors**

All finished sizes, yarn lengths, and fiberfill quantities are approximate.

1 **Make a slip knot.** Create a slip knot that has an 8" (20 cm) tail. Make the slip-knot loop about 1½" (3.8 cm) or two fingers wide.

2 **Make the chain.** Chain on a total of 12 loops for Row 1.

3 **Make a circle.** Make the chain row (Row 1) into a circle by pulling the tail yarn through loop 12 of the chain row.

4 **Row 2: Knit 12.** To start Row 2, have both the tail yarn and working yarn pointing away from you. With the working yarn, start pulling up loops through each top loop of the chain row, working to the right. As you pull up loops, pull the working yarn as close as possible to the last loop to keep your loops tight and close together.

5 **Rows 3 onward: Knit 12.** Once there are 12 loops pulled up in Row 2, continue working in the round and pulling up loops. Each new row will have 12 loops. Continue to pull up loops at a consistent size, about 1½" (3.8 cm) wide, ensuring that they are tight and close together.

**TIP:** Count each row as you go to keep track of how many rows you are at, or use a stitch marker to mark the beginning of each row. Another way to count is to keep track of your tail yarn: Once you knit a loop that is lined up with your tail yarn at the bottom of the project, knit one more loop over, and that will mark the end of the row. From there, you can count to see how many rows you have completed. Pull slightly on a row to see the separation of rows better.

6 **Add a new skein.** When you reach the end of your skein of yarn, attach a second skein by tying a knot on the inside of the project, behind the last loop pulled up. Make sure to cut the excess yarn off from the knot.

7 **Through Row 28: Knit 12.** Continue knitting 12 loops for each row until you have a total of 28 rows or until your pillow measures 18" (46 cm) long.

8 **Trim the yarn.** Cut the working yarn off the skein, leaving a tail of about 8" (20 cm) of working yarn.

**9** **Close the bottom of the pouf.** Pull the tail yarn (back at the starting end of the project) through each bottom loop from the outside toward the inside, working to the right and tightening gently as you go. Once finished, make a double knot at the base of the tail yarn and then push the tail yarn and knot through the center of the hole.

**10** **Stuff the pouf.** The amount of fiberfill you add will depend on how firm or soft you want your pillow to be. Make sure to start at the closed-off bottom and work your way up.

**TIP:** Don't overstuff the pillow, since too much stuffing might create more-significant gaps within the loops of the project. In finger-knit projects made with chunky yarn, you will often be able to see some of the fiberfill (that's the nature of the craft), but not overfilling your projects will help minimize these occurrences. It also helps a lot to make sure your loops are small, tight, and consistent in size!

**11** **Close the top of the pouf.** Pull the working yarn through each loop from the inside of the project toward the outside, working to the left. Once finished, make a double knot at the base of the working yarn and then push the working yarn and knot through the center of the hole.

**TIP:** The size and shape of this pillow are easily customizable! If you want to make a wider pillow, add more loops to the chain row; if you want to make a thinner pillow, add fewer loops to the chain row. If you want to make a shorter pillow, knit fewer rows; if you want to make a longer pillow, knit more rows.

***Finished Size:***
5" × 5" (12.7 × 12.7 cm)

***Skill Level:***
Beginner

# STRESS-BALL BUDDY

The Stress-Ball Buddy is the most straightforward stuffie project you can imagine: It's simply a little ball with eyes! It's another perfect foundational project that will help you get the hang of fundamental skills like knitting in the round, pulling up loops, and adding eyes to a project. It's perfect for beginners. (You can also check out a video tutorial for this Stress-Ball Buddy on my YouTube Channel!)

Once you start completing a number of different projects, you'll start to notice you have a lot of scrap yarn on hand. Don't stress over your pile of scraps—the Stress-Ball Buddy pattern is just what you need to help reduce stress *and* your scrap pile!

## SUPPLIES

**Chunky blanket yarn:**
Color of choice: 5½ yards (5 m)

**Fiberfill: ½ ounce (15 g)**

**Scissors**

All finished sizes, yarn lengths, and fiberfill quantities are approximate.

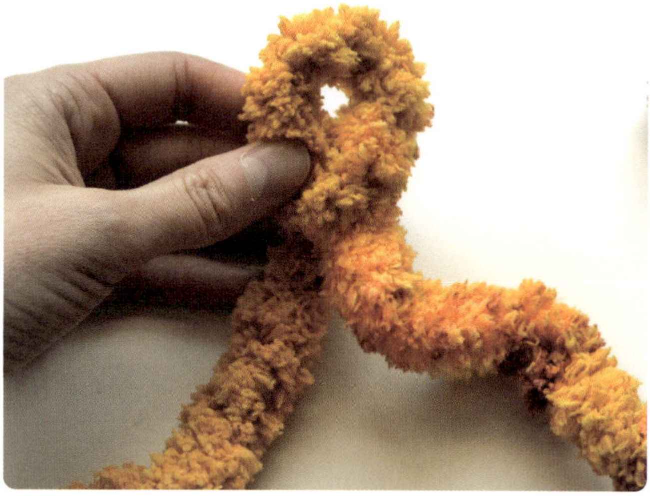

**1 Make a slip knot.** Create a slip knot that has an 8" (20 cm) tail. Make the slip-knot loop about 1½" (3.8 cm) or two fingers wide.

**2 Make the chain.** Chain on a total of 7 loops for Row 1.

**3 Make a circle.** Make the chain row (Row 1) into a circle by pulling the tail yarn through loop 7 of the chain row.

**4 Row 2: Knit 7.** With both the tail yarn and working yarn pointing away from you, start pulling up loops through each top loop of the chain row, working to the right. As you pull up loops, pull the working yarn as close as possible to the last loop to keep your loops tight and close together.

5 **Rows 3–7: Knit 7 (35 loops total).** Knit five more rows with 7 loops/stitches each—the same number of loops/stitches as Row 2.

**TIP:** Count each row as you go to keep track of how many rows you are at, or use a stitch marker to mark the beginning of each row. Another way to count is to keep track of your tail yarn: Once you knit a loop that is lined up with your tail yarn at the bottom of the project, knit one more loop over, and that will mark the end of the row. From there, you can count to see how many rows you have completed. Pull slightly on a row to see the separation of rows better.

6 **Trim the yarn.** Cut the working yarn off the skein, leaving a tail of about 8" (20 cm) of working yarn.

7 **Prepare the eyes.** Cut two 6" (16 cm) pieces of black yarn and tie a single knot at the center of each piece.

**8** **Add the eyes.** Add the eyes right in the middle of the stress ball, with one and a half columns between each eye. To add an eye, first thread the end of each eye strand to the inside of the ball, wrapping the ends around a single loop of yarn of the ball and leaving the eye knot itself sitting on the exterior of the ball. Then secure each eye by tying the eye-strand ends together on the inside of the ball.

**9** **Close the bottom of the ball.** Pull the tail yarn (back at the starting end of the project) through each bottom loop from the outside toward the inside, working to the right and tightening gently as you go. Once finished, make a double knot at the base of the tail yarn and then push the tail yarn and knot through the center of the hole.

**10** **Stuff the ball.** The amount of fiberfill you add will depend on how firm or soft you want your stress ball to be.

**11** **Close the top of the ball.** Pull the working yarn through each loop from the inside of the project toward the outside, working to the left. Once finished, make a double knot at the base of the working yarn and then push the working yarn and knot through the center of the hole.

***Finished Size:***
10" (25 cm) long

***Skill Level:***
Beginner

# BUMBLEBEE

Beatrice the Bumblebee is the stuffie that gave me the confidence to continue trying new patterns. I had attempted an octopus stuffie at first, but I just could not get the pattern down. When my sister asked me to make her a bumblebee stuffie, I was hesitant but decided to give it a go anyway. Off to Michaels we went to pick out the traditional bumblebee colors: yellow, black, and white. To my surprise, the pattern came out better than expected!

Since the original Beatrice the Bumblebee, I've continued to revise and improve the pattern and now offer it in three different sizes. For this pattern, I'll share my middle size. Now, let's get down to bees-ness!

## SUPPLIES

**Chunky blanket yarn:**
Yellow: 10 yards (9.1 m)
Black: 4 yards (3.7 m)
White: 2 yards (1.8 m)

**Fiberfill: 4 ounces (110 g)**

**Scissors**

All finished sizes, yarn lengths, and fiberfill quantities are approximate.

## BODY

**1 Make a slip knot.** With yellow yarn, create a slip knot that has an 8" (20 cm) tail. Make the slip-knot loop about 1½" (3.8 cm) or two fingers wide.

**2 Make the chain.** Chain on a total of 10 loops for Row 1.

**3 Make a circle.** Make the chain row (Row 1) into a circle by pulling the tail yarn through loop 10 of the chain row.

**4 Rows 2–3: Knit 10 (20 loops total).** With both the tail yarn and working yarn pointing away from you, start pulling up loops through each top loop of the chain row, working to the right. Complete two rows.

**5 Change to black.** Tie the black yarn onto the yellow with a double knot on the backside of the last loop (on the bee's inside), but don't cut the yellow yarn off like you normally would when changing colors. Trim the excess black yarn if needed.

**6 Rows 4–5: Knit 10 (20 loops total).** Start pulling up loops with the black yarn. Complete two rows with the black yarn.

**7 Change back to yellow.** After making the last loop of Row 5, place the yellow yarn under the black yarn so the yellow yarn is on the left side and the black yarn on the right side.

**8 Rows 6–7: Knit 10 (20 loops total).** Bring the yellow yarn up, cross it over the top of the black yarn tightly to the right, and start pulling up loops with the yellow yarn again. Complete two rows with the yellow yarn.

**9** **Rows 8–9: Knit 10 (20 loops total).** Repeat steps 7–8, but working with opposite colors, to switch back to black. That is, for this color switch, you are placing the black yarn under the yellow yarn so the black is on the left and the yellow is on the right, then bringing the black yarn up, crossing it over the top of the yellow yarn, etc. Complete two rows with the black yarn.

**10** **Finish with the black.** Cut the black yarn to a tail of about 6" (16 cm) long and tie a double knot onto the yellow yarn on the bee's inside. Trim the excess black yarn if needed.

**11** **Rows 10–13: Knit 10 (40 loops total).** Start pulling up loops with the yellow yarn again. Complete four rows with the yellow yarn. Then cut the yellow working yarn, leaving an 8" (20 cm) tail.

## WINGS (×2)

**12** **Make the chain.** With white yarn, make a slip knot and chain on a total of 4 loops that are about 1½" (3.8 cm) or two fingers wide each. Then, turn the yarn vertically so that the last loop is pointing up and away from you.

**13** **Add a side loop.** Pull up a fifth loop three loops down on the right side.

**14** **Pull a loop over the side loop.** Pull the top loop (loop 4) over the top of and down around the side loop (loop 5).

**15** **Add a side loop.** Pull up a sixth loop on the following loop down on the right side.

**16** **Pull a loop over this side loop.** Pull the previous loop (loop 5) over the top of and down around the new side loop just pulled up (loop 6).

**17** **Close the wing.** Cut the working yarn, leaving a 6" (16 cm) tail, and pull the yarn through loop 6 to close up the wing.

**18** **Place the wings.** Insert the two wings at the top of the bee, right at the middle yellow stripe. Space the wings just one column apart. There will be a slight slant in the wings; make sure they point the same way and toward the back of the bee (the tail yarn end).

**19** **Secure the wings.** On the bee's inside, double-knot the two strands of each respective wing to secure them to the body.

## EYES (×2) AND FINISHING

**20** **Close the top of the bee.** Pull the working yarn through each loop from the inside of the project toward the outside, working to the left. Once finished, tie a double knot at the base of the working yarn and then push the working yarn and knot through the center of the hole.

**21** **Add the eyes.** Cut two 6" (16 cm) pieces of black yarn and tie a single knot at the center of each piece. Insert each eye at the front of the bee, with the single knot on the inside and the two strands on the outside. Once the eyes are in place, tie a double knot with each strand, flip the double knots to the bee's inside, and push the single knot to the outside.

**22** **Stuff and close the bottom.** Stuff the bee. Pull the tail yarn through each bottom loop from the outside toward the inside, working to the right and tightening gently as you go. Once finished, tie a double knot at the base of the tail yarn and then push the tail yarn and knot through the center of the hole.

***Finished Size:***
10" × 9" (25 × 23 cm)

***Skill Level:***
Beginner

# HEN

I'm thrilled to share this versatile five-in-one pattern with you! This Hen pattern, which I named Harriet the Hen, is a great base, and I've modified it to make it adaptable for a whole flock of feathered friends. With just a few tweaks, you can transform Harriet the Hen into five different birds: Darla the Duck, Millie the Mallard, Edward the Eagle, and Flo the Flamingo. Once you've mastered the base pattern for the Hen, you'll have the confidence to customize and create any of the birds. There's no need to put all your eggs in one basket!

## SUPPLIES

**Chunky blanket yarn:**
White: 15 yards (13.7 m)
Yellow: 1½ yards (1.4 m)
Red: 1½ yards (1.4 m)
Black: 1 foot (30 cm)

**Fiberfill: 4 ounces (110 g)**

**Scissors**

All finished sizes, yarn lengths, and fiberfill quantities are approximate.

## BODY

1 **Make a slip knot.** With white (or primary-color) yarn, create a slip knot that has an 8" (20 cm) tail. Make the slip-knot loop about 1½" (3.8 cm) or two fingers wide.

2 **Make the chain.** Chain on a total of 10 loops for Row 1.

3 **Make a circle.** Make the chain row (Row 1) into a circle by pulling the tail yarn through loop 10 of the chain row.

4 **Row 2: Knit 10.** With both the tail yarn and working yarn pointing away from you, start pulling up loops through each top loop of the chain row, working to the right.

**5** **Rows 3–12: Knit 10 (100 loops total).** Continue knitting until you have knitted a total of 12 rows. Cut the working yarn, leaving about 8" (20 cm) tail of yarn.

## WINGS (×2)

**6** **Make the chain.** With white (or primary-color) yarn, make a slip knot and chain on a total of 3 loops, each about 1½" (3.8 cm) or two fingers wide. Then turn the yarn vertically so that the last loop is pointing up and away from you.

**7** **Add a side loop.** Pull up a fourth loop in the third loop down on the right side.

**8** **Pull a loop over this side loop.** Pull the top loop (loop 3) over the top of and down around the side loop (loop 4).

**9** **Close off the wing.** Close off the last loop you made by pulling the working yarn through it and tightening gently.

**10** **Place the wings horizontally.** Put both wings evenly on either side of the hen's body. There should be four columns between each wing on both sides.

**11** **Place the wings vertically.** Orient the wings about five rows down from the top of the hen's body, with the wings facing down. Pull the strands through to the inside of the body.

**12** **Secure the wings.** Tie a double knot on the inside of the body to secure each wing to the hen.

## EYES (×2)

**13** **Make the eyes.** Cut two 6" (16 cm) pieces of black yarn and tie a single knot at the center of each piece.

**14** **Add the eyes.** Place the eyes one column over from either wing, on the same side (that is, in between columns 1 and 2 and columns 3 and 4, as shown here). Tie a double knot on the inside of the body to secure each eye to the hen. (I like to place the eyes in line with the wings, but you can always adjust the placement on the basis of your preference.)

## BEAK

**15** **Make the beak.** With yellow yarn, make a slip knot and chain on a total of 2 loops. Close off the chain by pulling the working yarn through the last loop and then tightening it.

**16** **Place the beak.** With the beak oriented vertically, place the beak evenly between the two eyes and about one row below them. Tie a double knot on the inside of the body to secure the beak.

**17** **Close the top of the hen.** Pull the working yarn through each loop from the inside of the project toward the outside, working to the left. Once finished, make a double knot at the base of the working yarn and then push the working yarn and knot through the center of the hole.

## COMB

**18** **Make the comb.** With red yarn, make a slip knot and chain on a total of 6 loops. Close off the chain by pulling the working yarn through the last loop and then tightening it.

**19** **Place the comb.** At the top of the hen, place one end of the comb chain in front of the closed hole and one end of the comb chain behind the closed hole, aligning it vertically with the hen's face.

**20** **Secure the comb.** Pull up a red comb strand from the inside of the head to the outside, through the center of the top. Pull that strand through a bottom loop of the hen's comb. Now that the strand is on the opposite side, pull the strand back down into the center of the top. Finally, tie the two red strands together on the inside to secure. Make sure that you are tying the two red strands of yarn together—there are a lot of strands inside the hen at this point! Also make sure to tie the knot tightly and all the way at the top of the head (on the inside).

## FEET (×2) AND FINISHING

**21** **Make the feet.** With yellow yarn, make a slip knot and chain on a total of 2 loops. Close off the chain by pulling the working yarn through the last loop and then tightening it.

**22** **Secure the feet.** Insert the feet yarn strands one row up from the bottom, between the eyes and the wings. Tie a double knot on the inside of the body to secure each foot to the hen.

**23** **Stuff and close off.** Stuff the hen with fiberfill. Pull the tail yarn through each bottom loop from the outside toward the inside, working to the right and tightening gently as you go. Once finished, make a double knot at the base of the tail yarn and then push the tail yarn and knot through the center of the hole.

***Finished Size:***
10" × 9" (25 × 23 cm)

***Skill Level:***
Beginner

### *Hen Variation:*

# DUCK

Darla the Duck is different from Harriet the Hen in several ways! She has two-toned eyes, head fluff instead of a comb, and a horizontal beak.

If you need extra guidance while making any of the standard parts of this project, refer to the more detailed instructions for Hen on page 66!

## SUPPLIES

**Chunky blanket yarn:**
Yellow: 15 yards (13.7 m)
Orange: 1½ yards (1.4 m)
Black: 1 foot (30 cm)
White (optional): 1 foot (30 cm)

**Fiberfill: 4 ounces (110 g)**

**Scissors**

All finished sizes, yarn lengths, and fiberfill quantities are approximate.

## BODY

1 **Make the body.** With yellow yarn, create a slip knot that has an 8" (20 cm) tail. Chain on a total of 10 loops for Row 1. Make the loops about 1½" (3.8 cm) or two fingers wide. Make your chain row into a circle. Then knit standard rows as follows: Rows 2–12: Knit 10 (110 loops total). Finally, cut the working yarn, leaving about an 8" (20 cm) tail of yarn.

## WINGS (×2)

2 **Add wings.** With yellow yarn, make a slip knot and chain on a total of 3 loops. Turn the yarn vertically so that the last loop is pointing up and away from you. Pull up a fourth loop three loops down on the right side. Then pull the top loop (loop 3) over the top of and down around the side loop (loop 4). Cut the working yarn, leaving a 6" (16 cm) tail. Close off the chain by pulling the working yarn through the last loop. Attach both wings facing down on either side of the duck's body, with four columns between each wing and about five rows down from the top of the body.

## EYES (×2)

3 **Start the eyes.** Cut two 6" (16 cm) pieces of black yarn and tie a single knot at the center of each piece. Add the eyes to the body one column over from either wing on the same side. Tie them on the inside of the duck to secure them. Then cut two 6" (16 cm) pieces of white yarn and place one piece to the left of the left eye and one piece to the right of the right eye.

4 **Finish the eyes.** Pull the white yarn past the knot of each black eye, so just a little bit of white yarn is peeking out, then tie the white yarn with a double knot inside the duck to secure it.

## BEAK

5 **Add the beak.** With orange yarn, make a slip knot and chain on a total of 3 loops. Close off the chain by pulling the working yarn through the last loop. With the beak oriented horizontally, place the beak between the two eyes and about one row below the eyes. Close off the top of the duck, following the standard closing instructions.

## FEET (×2)

6 **Add feet.** With orange yarn, make a slip knot and chain on a total of 2 loops. Close off the chain by pulling the working yarn through the last loop. Insert the yarn strands one row up from the bottom, between the eyes and the wings. Secure the feet by tying their strands in a double knot inside the duck.

## HEAD FLUFF AND FINISHING

7 **Start the fluff.** Cut two 10" (25 cm) pieces of yellow yarn. At the top of the head, slide the pieces of yarn evenly under the center of the closed hole, with one piece going vertically across the head and the other going horizontally.

8 **Finish the fluff and the duck.** Tie a single knot with each piece, grabbing the piece across from it. Do this twice, making the last knot a double knot. Trim the head fluff to your preferred length. Stuff the duck with fiberfill and then close the bottom of the duck, following the standard closing instructions.

***Finished Size:***
9" × 9" (23 × 23 cm)

***Skill Level:***
Beginner

*Hen Variation:*

# MALLARD

Millie the Mallard will give you a chance to adapt the basic form of Harriet the Hen, but in a multicolor design to mimic the various colors of her namesake mallard.

If you need extra guidance while making any of the standard parts of this project, refer to the more detailed instructions for Hen on page 66!

## SUPPLIES

**Chunky blanket yarn:**
Brown: 7 yards (6.4 m)
Green: 6 yards (5.5 m)
White: 2½ yards (2.3 m)
Yellow: 1½ yards (1.4 m)
Black: 1 foot (30 cm)

**Fiberfill: 4 ounces (110 g)**

**Scissors**

All finished sizes, yarn lengths, and fiberfill quantities are approximate.

## BODY

1 **Start the body.** With brown yarn, create a slip knot that has an 8" (20 cm) tail. Chain on a total of 10 loops for Row 1. Make the loops about 1½" (3.8 cm) or two fingers wide. Make your chain row into a circle. Then knit standard rows as follows: Rows 2–5: Knit 10 (40 loops total).

2 **Change to white.** Change the color to white by tying a knot onto the brown yarn inside the project, right after the last loop of Row 5. Trim the excess yarn on the knot, keeping the white yarn attached to continue with. Then knit standard rows as follows: Rows 6–7: Knit 10 (20 loops total).

3 **Change to green.** Change the color to green by tying a knot onto the white yarn inside the project, right after the last loop of Row 7. Trim the excess yarn on the knot, keeping the green yarn attached to continue with. Then knit standard rows as follows: Rows 8–12: Knit 10 (50 loops total). Finally, cut the working yarn, leaving a tail of about 8" (20 cm).

## WINGS (×2)

4 **Add wings.** With brown yarn, make a slip knot and chain on a total of 3 loops. Turn the yarn vertically so that the last loop is pointing up and away from you. Pull up a fourth loop three loops down on the right side. Pull the top loop (loop 3) over the top of and down around the side loop (loop 4). Cut the working yarn, leaving a 6" (16 cm) tail. Close off the chain by pulling the working yarn through the last loop and then tightening it. Attach both wings facing down on either side of the mallard's body, right at the bottom row of the white stripe, with four rows between each wing.

## EYES (×2)

**5** **Add eyes.** Cut two 6" (16 cm) pieces of black yarn and tie a single knot at the center of each piece. Add the eyes in the green section of the mallard, one column over from each wing and one row above the white stripe. Tie a double knot on the inside of the body to secure each eye to the body.

## BEAK

**6** **Add a beak.** With yellow yarn, make a slip knot and chain on a total of 3 loops. Close off the chain by pulling the working yarn through the last loop and then tightening it. With the beak oriented horizontally, place the beak evenly between the two eyes and about one row below them. Close the top of the mallard, following the standard closing instructions.

## FEET AND FINISHING

**7** **Add feet and finish.** With yellow yarn, make a slip knot and chain on a total of 2 loops. Close off the chain by pulling the working yarn through the last loop and then tightening it. Add the feet one row up from the bottom and in the column between the eyes and the wings. Tie a double knot on the inside of the body to secure each foot to the body. Stuff the mallard with fiberfill and then close the bottom of the mallard, following the standard closing instructions.

***Finished Size:***
10" × 9" (25 × 23 cm)

***Skill Level:***
Beginner

***Hen Variation:***

# EAGLE

Edward the Eagle has a unique head-to-body ratio compared to Harriet the Hen, with a subtle but special collar dividing the two.

If you need extra guidance while making any of the standard parts of this project, refer to the more detailed instructions for Hen on page 66!

## SUPPLIES

**Chunky blanket yarn:**
Dark brown: 7 yards (6.4 m)
White: 10 yards (9.1 m)
Yellow: 1½ yards (1.4 m)
Black: 1 foot (30 cm)

**Fiberfill: 4 ounces (110 g)**

**Scissors**

All finished sizes, yarn lengths, and fiberfill quantities are approximate.

## BODY

1 **Start the body.** With dark-brown yarn, create a slip knot that has an 8" (20 cm) tail. Chain on a total of 10 loops for Row 1. Make the loops about 1½" (3.8 cm) or two fingers wide. Make your chain row into a circle. Then knit standard rows as follows: Rows 2–5: Knit 10 (40 loops total). Now change the color to white by tying a knot onto the dark-brown yarn inside the project, right after the last loop of Row 5. Trim the excess yarn on the knot, keeping the white yarn attached to continue with.

2 **Row 6: Close off all the loops.** To make Row 6, treat the row as if it is a closing row, where you have 2 loops up and then close the first loop made off with the second loop in the row. So, to start, pull up 2 loops as shown . . .

3 **Row 6 (continued).** . . . and then pull the first loop over the top of and down around the second loop. Continue this pattern until you have only 1 loop left in the row.

4 **Row 7: Increase 1.** In the next space over, to the right of the single white loop from Row 6, increase 1. This should be right at the knot where you changed colors. Then close off that loop too, so that you again are left with a single loop.

5 **Row 7 (continued) and Rows 8–12.** To complete Row 7, knit nine more standard stitches by pulling up new loops on each inside loop. Then knit standard rows as follows: Rows 8–12: Knit 10 (50 loops total). Cut the working yarn, leaving about an 8" (20 cm) tail of yarn.

## WINGS (×2)

6 **Add wings.** With dark-brown yarn, make a slip knot and chain on a total of 3 loops. Then, turn the yarn vertically so that the last loop is pointing up and away from you. Pull up a fourth loop three loops down on the right side. Pull the top loop (loop 3) over the top of and down around the side loop (loop 4). Cut the working yarn, leaving a 6" (16 cm) tail. Close off the chain by pulling the working yarn through the last loop and then tightening it. Attach both wings facing down on either side of the eagle's body, with four columns between them and placed right underneath the closed-off row of loops.

## EYES (×2)

7 **Add eyes.** Cut two 6" (16 cm) pieces of black yarn and tie a single knot at the center of each piece. Add the eyes one column over from each wing. Tie a double knot on the inside of the body to secure each eye to the body.

## BEAK

8 **Add the beak.** With yellow yarn, make a slip knot—effectively, a chain with just 1 loop. Close off the chain by pulling the working yarn through the slip-knot loop and then tightening it. With the beak oriented vertically, place the beak between the two eyes and about one row below them.

## COLLAR

9 **Start the collar.** Cut a 2½-foot (76 cm) piece of white yarn. Insert about 2" (5 cm) of one end into the eagle's body right at one of the closed-off loops around the neck.

10 **Continue the collar.** Wrap the rest of the yarn around each closed-off loop around the outside of the eagle's body.

**11** **Finish the collar.** Once you have gone all the way around, insert the excess yarn into the inside of the eagle's body (in a different hole than the other end of it), then tie a double knot with it to secure it in place. Close the top of the eagle, following the standard closing instructions.

## FEET AND FINISHING

**12** **Add feet and close up.** With yellow yarn, make a slip knot and chain on a total of 2 loops. Close off the chain by pulling the working yarn through the last loop and then tightening it. Add the feet one row up from the bottom and in the column between the eyes and the wings. Secure them in place with a double knot. Stuff the eagle with fiberfill and then close the bottom of the eagle, following the standard closing instructions.

***Finished Size:***
10" × 9" (25 × 23 cm)

***Skill Level:***
Beginner

*Hen Variation:*

# FLAMINGO

Flo the Flamingo's elaborate beak is what makes her stand out in a crowd. It's amazing how one iconic detail can really "sell" the species!

If you need extra guidance while making any of the standard parts of this project, refer to the more detailed instructions for Hen on page 66!

## SUPPLIES

**Chunky blanket yarn:**
Light pink: 7½ feet (228 cm)
Hot pink: 8 feet (243 cm)
Black: 1½ yards (1.4 m)
White: 1½ yards (1.4 m)

**Fiberfill: 4 ounces (110 g)**

**Scissors**

All finished sizes, yarn lengths, and fiberfill quantities are approximate.

## BODY

1 **Start the body.** With hot-pink yarn, create a slip knot that has an 8" (20 cm) tail. Chain on a total of 10 loops for Row 1. Make the loops about 1½" (3.8 cm) or two fingers wide. Make your chain row into a circle. Then knit standard rows as follows: Rows 2–6: Knit 10 (50 loops total). Finally, cut the working yarn, leaving about an 8" (20 cm) tail.

2 **Change colors.** Change the color to light pink by tying a knot onto the hot-pink yarn on the inside of the project, right after the last loop of Row 6. Trim the excess yarn on the knot, keeping the light-pink yarn attached to continue with. Then knit standard rows as follows: Rows 7–12: Knit 10 (60 loops total).

## WINGS (×2)

3 **Add the wings.** With hot-pink yarn, make a slip knot and chain on a total of 3 loops. Turn the yarn vertically so that the last loop is pointing up and away from you. Pull up a fourth loop three loops down on the right side. Pull the top loop (loop 3) over the top of and down around the side loop (loop 4). Cut the working yarn, leaving a 6" (16 cm) tail. Close off the chain by pulling the working yarn through the last loop and then tightening it. Attach both wings facing down on each side of the flamingo's body, placed right at the color change, with four columns between each wing.

## EYES (×2)

4 **Add the eyes.** Cut two 6" (16 cm) pieces of black yarn and tie a single knot at the center of each piece. Add the eyes one column over from either wing on the same side. Tie a double knot on the inside of the body to secure each eye to the flamingo. If desired, you can also add white to the eyes, as done for the Duck (see page 76).

## BEAK

**5** **Start the beak.** With black yarn, make a slip knot and chain on a total of 3 loops. Close off the chain by pulling the working yarn through the last loop and then tightening it. With the beak oriented vertically, place the beak between the two eyes and about one row below the eyes. Tie to secure.

**6** **Add white to the beak.** Cut a 10" (25 cm) piece of white yarn. Push one end of the yarn through the top of the flamingo's beak and into the inside of the body, leaving about 8" (20 cm) on the outside.

**7** **Finish the beak.** Wrap the yarn around the back of the beak twice, keeping it snug against the outside of the flamingo's body. Then push the remaining length of the wrapping end of the yarn into the inside of the flamingo's body at a different spot from where the first end was inserted. Tie the two ends of the yarn together inside the flamingo's body to secure it in place.

## FEET AND FINISHING

**8** **Add feet and close up.** With light-pink yarn, make a slip knot and chain on a total of 2 loops. Close off the chain by pulling the working yarn through the last loop and then tightening it. Insert the feet one row up from the bottom and in the column between the eyes and the wings. Tie the feet in place with a double knot. Close the top of the flamingo, following the standard closing instructions. Stuff the flamingo with fiberfill and then close the bottom of the flamingo, following the standard closing instructions.

***Finished Size:***
6" × 6" (15 × 15 cm)

***Skill Level:***
Confident Beginner

# OCTOPUS

Ollie the Octopus was the very first stuffie I ever made, and it quickly became one of my most-loved creations—especially at craft fairs! Including Ollie in this beginner-friendly book was a must, but I also wanted to give the original design a fresh twist. At first, I considered giving Ollie longer tentacles, but the charm of his short tentacles is undeniable, so I began brainstorming new ways to reimagine them. That's when inspiration struck: What if I used my new bobble stitch for the tentacles? Excited, I gave the idea a try, and, after several attempts—seven, to be exact—Ollie the Octopus 2.0 was born! The pattern is now perfected and ready to share with the world. With eight arms and endless charm, this Octopus pattern is sure to reel you in!

## SUPPLIES

**Chunky blanket yarn:**
Purple: 8½ yards (7.8 m)
Black: 1 foot (30 cm)

**Fiberfill: 1 ounce (28 g)**

**Scissors**

All finished sizes, yarn lengths, and fiberfill quantities are approximate.

## BODY

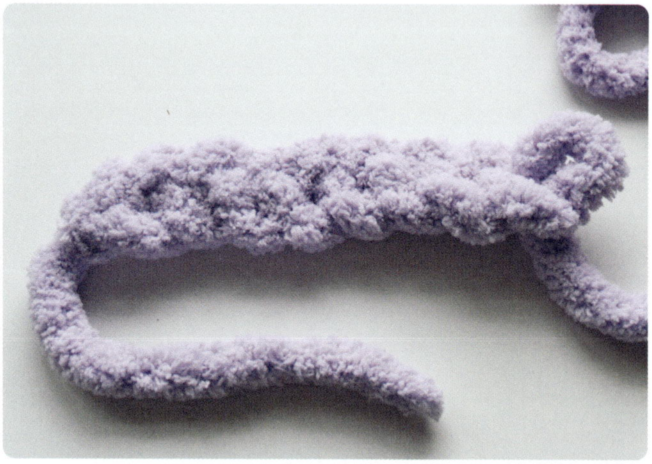

**1 Start the body.** With purple yarn, create a slip knot that has an 8" (20 cm) tail. Make the slip-knot loop about 1½" (3.8 cm) or two fingers wide. Chain on a total of 8 loops for Row 1. Make the chain row (Row 1) into a circle by pulling the tail yarn through loop 8 of the chain row.

**2 Rows 2–5: Knit 8 (32 loops total).** Knit standard rows as follows: Rows 2–5: Knit 8 (32 loops total).

**3 Row 6: Knit 3, decrease, knit 3, decrease (6 loops left).** For Row 6, first knit 3 loops like normal. Then, for the fourth loop, decrease by taking the fourth loop and pulling it over the top of and down around the third loop. Next, knit 3 again like normal. Finally, take the last loop of the row and decrease it by pulling it over the top of and down around the previous loop pulled up. This completes Row 6. Proceed to also knit another standard row as follows: Row 7: Knit 6.

**4 Row 8: Increase 1 and make a bobble, bobble 3, increase 1 and make a bobble, bobble 3 (8 bobbles total).** For Row 8, you'll be both increasing and making bobbles. See page 95 for the instructions on how to make a single bobble. Where the instructions here say "increase 1 and make a bobble," you should increase by pulling up a loop between the last loop made and the next loop, and then, working into the increase, make a bobble.

## HOW TO MAKE A BOBBLE

1 **Make a loop.** Knit 1 like normal or as an increase, depending on the project's specific instructions for that row. For example, Row 8 of this Octopus, as described in step 4 and shown here, starts with an increase, not a normal knit stitch.

2 **Move the working yarn.** Bring the working yarn to the outside of the project, on the right side of the loop just made.

3 **Make an additional loop.** On the right side of the loop just made, push up a second loop, from the front of the project to the back, in the same loop below that you pulled up the first loop.

4 **Move the working yarn.** Bring the working yarn back to the inside of the project, on the right side of the two loops just made. My thumb is through the two loops in this photo.

5 **Decrease the two loops.** Decrease the two loops by sandwiching them together and, with your working yarn, pulling up a new loop through both of them. Make sure to pull from the right side of the loops to the left side. You will be left with 1 loop.

6 **Check your work.** Here is one finished bobble. For the Octopus, after making this first bobble, continue making bobbles by following the pattern of Row 8 as explained in step 4 on page 94.

## FINISHING

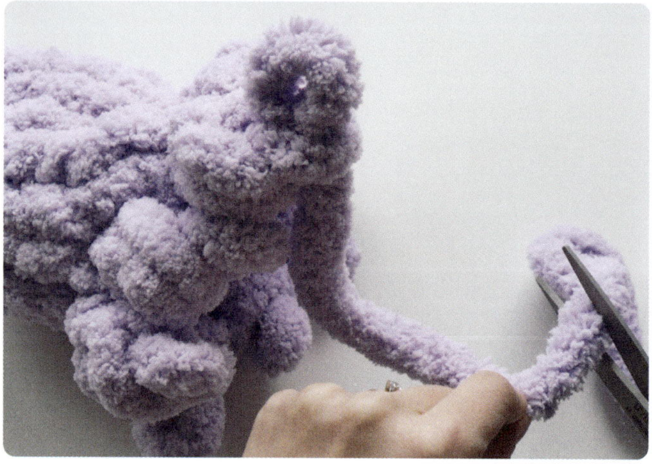

**5 Complete the body.** After you finish your eighth and final bobble of Row 8 as described in step 4 on page 94, knit 1 more loop onto the last loop pulled up (kind of like you are chaining on 1 more loop to the last loop). Then cut the working yarn, leaving about an 8" (20 cm) tail of yarn.

**6 Add the eyes.** Cut two 6" (16 cm) pieces of black yarn and tie a single knot at the center of each piece. Insert the eyes on the row above the bobbles, just one column apart. Tie a double knot on the inside of the body to secure each eye to the octopus.

**7 Close the bottom of the octopus.** Pull the working yarn through each loop from the inside of the project toward the outside, working to the left. Once finished, make a double knot at the base of the working yarn and then push the working yarn and knot through the center of the hole.

**8 Stuff and close up.** Stuff the octopus with fiberfill. Then close the top of the octopus: Pull the tail yarn through each bottom loop from the outside toward the inside, working to the right and tightening gently as you go. Once finished, make a double knot at the base of the tail yarn and then push the tail yarn and knot through the center of the hole.

**TIP:** Gently pull on the bobble stitches to bring them out and make them more visible.

***Finished Size:***
10" (25 cm) long

***Skill Level:***
Confident Beginner

# PICKLE

I was pleasantly surprised to discover just how popular pickle stuffies are! If you love pickles, then Petunia the Pickle is perfect for you. The pattern features the bobble stitch, which is ideal for creating the bumpy texture of a pickle. Positioning the bobbles just right took some trial and error, but once everything came together, the result was perfect. This pattern also includes an optional touch of creativity: You can add a bit of white around the eyes to make them stand out, and a slight blush of pink for extra charm. You'll relish every stitch of this pickle pattern!

## SUPPLIES

**Chunky blanket yarn:**
Green: 12 yards (11 m)
Black: 1 foot (30 cm)
White (optional): 1 foot (30 cm)
Pink (optional): 1 foot (30 cm)

**Fiberfill. 2½ ounces (70 g)**

**Scissors**

All finished sizes, yarn lengths, and fiberfill quantities are approximate.

## BODY

**1 Start the body.** With green yarn, create a slip knot that has an 8" (20 cm) tail. Make the slip-knot loop about 1½" (3.8 cm) or two fingers wide. Chain on a total of 8 loops for Row 1. Make the chain row (Row 1) into a circle by pulling the tail yarn through loop 8 of the chain row.

**2 Row 2: Knit 8.** With both the tail yarn and working yarn pointing away from you, start pulling up loops through each top loop of the chain row, working to the right. Knit a standard row of 8 stitches this way.

**3 Knit the rest of the body.** Knit rows as follows. This photo shows Row 3 completed. Refer to the bobble instructions on page 95 for a refresher on how to knit bobbles.

**Row 3:** Knit 5, bobble 1, knit 2.

**Row 4:** Knit 3, bobble 1, knit 4.

**Row 5:** Knit 7, bobble 1.

**Row 6:** Knit 8.

**Row 7:** Knit 1, bobble 1, knit 6.

**Row 8:** Knit 6, bobble 1, knit 1.

**Row 9:** Knit 8.

**Row 10:** Knit 4, bobble 1, knit 3.

**Row 11:** Bobble 1, knit 7.

**Row 12:** Knit 8.

**Row 13:** Knit 2, bobble 1, knit 5.

**Row 14:** Knit 8. Then cut the working yarn, leaving about an 8" (20 cm) tail of yarn.

## EYES (×2) AND CHEEKS (×2)

4 **Add the eyes.** Cut two 6" (16 cm) pieces of black yarn and tie a single knot at the center of each piece. You will insert each eye on the front of the pickle where there is space for them between the bobbles. Use the tail yarn to orient yourself: The tail yarn sits on the backside of the pickle. Place the eyes in line with the right bobble and one and a half columns apart. Use the knot-and-slide method described in Bee, step 21 (page 65). If desired, you can also add white to the eyes, as done for the Duck (see page 76).

5 **Add the cheeks.** Cut two 6" (16 cm) pieces of pink yarn and insert them one row below the eyes through just one loop and to the outer side of each eye. Tie a double knot with the yarn on the outside of the pickle and then flip the knots to the inside, leaving just a line of pink yarn visible on the outside.

## FINISHING

6 **Close the top of the pickle.** Pull the tail yarn through each bottom loop from the outside toward the inside, working to the right and tightening gently as you go. Once finished, make a double knot at the base of the tail yarn and then push the tail yarn and knot through the center of the hole.

7 **Stuff and close up.** Stuff the pickle with fiberfill. Then close the bottom of the pickle: Pull the working yarn through each loop from the inside of the project toward the outside, working to the left. Once finished, make a double knot at the base of the working yarn and then push the working yarn and knot through the center of the hole.

***Finished Size:***
8" × 7" (20 × 18 cm)

***Skill Level:***
Beginner

# WHALE

The original Willie the Whale pattern, available in both large and mini sizes, has been a favorite for quite some time—and for good reason! It's a splendid beginner-friendly stuffie. I decided to give it a fresh update for this book by redesigning the tail and giving it a new size. I'm calling this version the small Willie the Whale. Even though it's technically the middle size between the mini and large patterns, it's just too cute and petite to call "medium," so "small" it is! But that's not all—this updated pattern is also a four-in-one! I'm excited to show you how to take this Whale pattern to the next level and transform it into Sherwin the Shark, Wallace the Walrus, and Sheila the Seal. Let's dive in!

## SUPPLIES

**Chunky blanket yarn:**
Blue: 12 yards (11 m)
White: 5½ yards (5 m)
Black: 1 foot (30 cm)

**Fiberfill: 2 ounces (55 g)**

**Scissors**

All finished sizes, yarn lengths, and fiberfill quantities are approximate.

## BODY

1 **Start the body.** With white yarn, create a slip knot that has an 8" (20 cm) tail. Make the slip-knot loop about 1½" (3.8 cm) or two fingers wide. Chain on a total of 10 loops for Row 1. Make the chain row (Row 1) into a circle by pulling the tail yarn through loop 10 of the chain row.

2 **Rows 2–4: Knit 10 (30 loops total).** Knit standard rows as follows: Rows 2–4: Knit 10 (30 loops total).

3 **Change colors.** Tie the blue yarn onto the white yarn with a double knot, trim the excess yarn around the knot, and cut off the white.

4 **Rows 5–11: Knit 10 (70 loops total).** Knit standard rows as follows: Rows 5–11: Knit 10 (70 loops total). Then cut the working yarn, leaving about an 8" (20 cm) tail of yarn.

## TAIL

5 **Make the chain.** With blue yarn, create a slip knot that has an 8" (20 cm) tail. Chain on a total of 3 loops.

6 **Add a top loop.** Keeping the chain horizontal and now working to the left, pull up a new loop in the first loop so you have 2 loops total (one that is new from the first loop, and one that is the existing third loop of the chain).

7 **Continue chaining.** In the left loop, chain on 2 more loops, then cut the working yarn, leaving about a 15" (38 cm) tail.

8 **Close the left side.** Close off the long left-side chain by pulling the excess yarn through the last loop made and tightening it gently to close.

**9** **Weave the excess yarn.** Weave the excess yarn down the right side of the chain, going from the back and to the front of the tail, and then bring it over to the right loop.

**10** **Continue chaining.** Chain on 2 more loops on the right side, then close off the chain.

**11** **Weave the excess yarn.** Weave the excess yarn down the right side of the chain until it is at the bottom of the right side.

**12** **Finish the tail.** Finally, pull the tail yarn (not the excess yarn you've been weaving up till now) through the row above it on the left side so that is it even with the excess yarn on the right side.

13 **Place the tail.** Insert the strands of the tail around one column of the body, right at the first section of blue, with the tail oriented horizontally (parallel to the color line). Tie a single knot on the inside of the body to secure the tail to the whale.

14 **Continue attaching the tail.** Pop out one strand from the tail directly underneath the tail, then push it through the bottom center of the tail to the other side.

15 **Finish attaching the tail.** Bring the strand back inside the whale from directly above the tail. Make a double knot with both strands to secure everything in place on the inside of the whale.

## FINS (×2)

16 **Make the fins.** The fins are the same as the birds' wings; if needed, refer to page 69 for a refresher on how to make them. Here's a summary: With blue yarn, make a slip knot and chain on a total of 3 loops. Then, turn the yarn vertically so that the last loop is pointing up and away from you. Pull up a fourth loop three loops down on the right side. Pull the top loop (loop 3) over the top of and down around the side loop (loop 4). Cut the working yarn, leaving a 6" (16 cm) tail, and pull the yarn through the fourth loop to close up the fin.

17 **Add the fins.** Insert the fins one and a half columns to either side of the tail. The fins should be oriented horizontally and placed on the first row of blue, just like the tail. Tie a double knot on the inside of the body to secure each fin to the body.

## EYES (×2)

18 **Add the eyes.** Cut two 6" (16 cm) pieces of black yarn and tie a single knot at the center of each piece. Insert the eyes half a column from the fins on each side, on the first row of blue. Tie a double knot on the inside of the body to secure each eye to the whale.

## FINISHING

19 **Close the bottom of the whale.** Pull the tail yarn through each bottom loop from the outside toward the inside, working to the right and tightening gently as you go. Once finished, make a double knot at the base of the tail yarn and then push the tail yarn and knot through the center of the hole.

20 **Stuff and close up.** Stuff the whale with fiberfill. Then close the top of the whale: Pull the working yarn through each loop from the inside of the project toward the outside, working to the left. Once finished, make a double knot at the base of the working yarn and then push the working yarn and knot through the center of the hole.

***Finished Size:***
9" × 9" (23 × 23 cm)

***Skill Level:***
Beginner

### *Whale Variation:*

# SHARK

Sherwin the Shark is a predator! You can tell by his sharp dorsal fin and matching vertical tailfin, which make him stand out from gentler Willie the Whale.

If you need extra guidance while making any of the standard parts of this project, refer to the more detailed instructions for Whale on page 102!

## SUPPLIES

**Chunky blanket yarn:**
Dark gray: 15 yards (13.7 m)
White: 5 yards (4.6 m)
Black: 1 foot (30 cm)

**Fiberfill: 2 ounces (55 g)**

**Scissors**

All finished sizes, yarn lengths, and fiberfill quantities are approximate.

Shark

## BODY

**1 Make the body.** Refer to steps 1–4 of Whale (page 104) for how to make the shark body—the only difference is when you change colors. For the Shark, knit just three total rows of white (Rows 1–3, 30 loops total), then change to dark gray and knit eight more rows (Rows 4–11, 80 loops total). Cut the working yarn, leaving about 8" (20 cm) of yarn.

## TAIL

**2 Make the tail.** Refer to steps 5–12 of Whale (page 105) for how to make the tail—the only difference is that you're using dark-gray yarn.

**3 Attach the tail.** Refer to steps 13–15 of Whale (page 107) for how to attach the tail—the only difference is that you should orient the tail vertically instead of horizontally (perpendicular to the color line).

## FINS (×2)

**4 Make the fins.** With dark-gray yarn, make a slip knot and chain on a total of 3 loops. Turn the yarn vertically so that the last loop is pointing up and away from you. Pull up a fourth loop three loops down on the right side. Pull the top loop (loop 3) over the top of and down around the side loop (loop 4). Cut the working yarn, leaving a 6" (16 cm) tail, and pull the yarn through the fourth loop to close up the fin.

5 **Add the fins.** Insert the fins one and a half columns to either side of the tail. The fins should be oriented horizontally (perpendicular to the tail) and be placed on the second row up on the dark gray. Tie a double knot on the inside of the body to secure each fin to the shark.

## EYES (×2)

6 **Add eyes and close up.** Cut two 6" (16 cm) pieces of black yarn and tie a single knot at the center of each piece. Insert the eyes half a column over from the fins on each side. Tie a double knot on the inside of the body to secure each eye to the shark. Close the bottom of the shark, following the standard instructions (work to the right, pulling from the outside to the inside). Stuff the shark with fiberfill. Then close the top of the shark, following the standard instructions (work to the left, pulling from the inside to the outside).

## DORSAL FIN AND FINISHING

7 **Start the dorsal fin.** Grab your skein of dark gray yarn again. At the top of the shark's head, pull up 2 loops that are aligned with the tail and the center of the face. Pull the first loop up in front of the closed-up hole, leaving a 6" (16 cm) tail of yarn, and pull up the second loop behind it. (Note: In the photos, the second loop is pulled up to the left of the first loop because the shark is turned to the side, with the face pointing to the right and the tail pointing to the left. In the following steps, "back" refers to the tail side and "front" refers to the face side.)

8 **Knit 2.** Knit 2 loops: one in the back and then one in the front.

9 **Knit 1.** Knit 1 in the front loop.

10 **Decrease.** Decrease by pulling the front loop you just made through the back loop. You'll be left with 1 loop.

11 **Knit 1.** Knit 1 more loop to complete the dorsal-fin shape. Then cut your working yarn to about 8" (20 cm) and close the loop.

**12** **Weave in the excess.** Weave the excess yarn down the backside of the dorsal fin (pulling it downward as you go, so the fin points backward toward the tail). Then, weave the yarn through the bottom of the fin to reach the tail yarn.

**13** **Finish with a knot.** Tie a double knot with the tail yarn and working yarn. Stuff the knot and excess yarn inside the shark.

***Finished Size:***
10" × 6" (25 × 15 cm)

***Skill Level:***
Confident Beginner

*Whale Variation:*

# WALRUS

Wallace the Walrus is unique from the other sea creatures due mainly to his protruding mouth and tusks. He also features two-toned eyes that give him a sweet look.

If you need extra guidance while making any of the standard parts of this project, refer to the more detailed instructions for Whale on page 102!

## SUPPLIES

**Chunky blanket yarn:**
Brown: 15 yards (13.7 m)
Black: 1 foot (30 cm)
White: 2 feet (61 cm)

**Fiberfill: 2 ounces (55 g)**

**Scissors**

All finished sizes, yarn lengths, and fiberfill quantities are approximate.

## BODY

**1 Start the body.** With brown yarn, create a slip knot that has an 8" (20 cm) tail. Make the slip-knot loop about 1½" (3.8 cm) or two fingers wide. Chain on a total of 10 loops for Row 1. Make the chain row (Row 1) into a circle by pulling the tail yarn through loop 10 of the chain row. Then knit standard rows as follow: Rows 2–3: Knit 10 (20 loops total).

## HOW TO MAKE A REVERSE BOBBLE

**1 Row 4: Knit 3, bobble 1, reverse bobble 1, knit 5.** To continue to Row 4, you'll need to learn how to make a reverse bobble, as explained here and in the following steps. First, start the row by knitting 3 and bobbling 1 as stated. Then, to start the reverse bobble, knit 1 like normal. Next, bring the working yarn to the outside of the project, on the right side of the loop just made. On the right side of the loop just made, push up a second loop, from the front of the project to the back, in the same loop below that you pulled up the first loop. (So far, this is just like a regular bobble.)

**2 Move the working yarn.** Bring the working yarn back to the inside of the project, on the left side of the two loops just made. My right index finger is through the two loops in this photo. (This is the same as a regular bobble except that you are bringing your working yarn to the left side of the two loops this time, instead of to the right.)

3 **Decrease the two loops.** Decrease the two loops by sandwiching them together and, with your working yarn, pulling up a new loop through both of them. Make sure to pull from the left side of the loops to the right side. You will be left with 1 loop. (This the same as a regular bobble except that you are decreasing from the left to the right, instead of from the right to the left.).

4 **Check your work.** Here is the finished reverse bobble next to the regular bobble. The regular bobble is on the left side, pointing to the right, and the reverse bobble is on the right side, pointing to the left. The working yarn is now on the inside of the project and on the left side of the reverse bobble. To continue knitting like normal, bring the working yarn to the next loop in the row by pulling the working yarn to the right side of the reverse bobble, keeping the working yarn on the inside of the project. Complete Row 4 by knitting 5.

## BODY (CONTINUED)

2 **Rows 5–10: Knit 10 (60 loops total).** Knit standard rows as follows: Rows 5–10: Knit 10 (60 loops total).

## TAIL

3 **Make the tail.** Refer to steps 5–12 of Whale (page 105) for how to make the tail—the only difference is that you're using brown yarn and that when you weave the excess yarn down the right side of the chain, weave until it is one row up from the tail yarn.

4 **Attach the tail.** Refer to steps 13–15 of Whale (page 107) for how to attach the tail—the only difference is that you should place the tail horizontally in between a column (the column the tail yarn is lined up with), three rows up from the bottom.

## FINS (×2)

5 **Make the fins.** With brown yarn, make a slip knot and chain on a total of 3 loops. Turn the yarn vertically so that the last loop is pointing up and away from you. Pull up a fourth loop three loops down on the right side. Pull the top loop (loop 3) over the top and down the side loop (loop 4). Cut the working yarn, leaving a 6" (16 cm) tail, and pull the yarn through the fourth loop to close up the fin.

6 **Add the fins.** Insert the fins one and a half columns to each side of the tail. They should be oriented horizontally and placed on the third row up from the bottom, in line with the tail. Tie a double knot on the inside of the body to secure each fin to the body.

## NOSE

7 **Add the nose.** Cut an 8" (20 cm) piece of black yarn and wrap it twice around the center row, right above the two bobbles, to create the nose. On opposite sides of the nose, put both black strands on the inside of the walrus and tie a double knot to secure them in place.

## EYES (×2) AND FINISHING

8 **Add eyes.** Cut two 6" (16 cm) pieces of black yarn and tie a single knot at the center of each piece. Insert the eyes one column over from the fins (one column to the side and one row above the bobbles). Tie a double knot on the inside of the body to secure each eye to the body. If desired, add white to the eyes too. Cut two 6" (16 cm) pieces of white yarn and place the strands to the outer side of each eye (to the left of the left eye and to the right of the right eye). Pull the yarn past the knot of the eye, so just a little bit of white yarn is peeking out, then tie the pieces on the inside to secure them.

9 **Close up the project.** Close the bottom of the walrus, following the standard instructions (work to the right, pulling from the outside to the inside). Stuff the walrus with fiberfill. Then close the top of the walrus, following the standard instructions (work to the left, pulling from the inside to the outside).

## TUSKS

10 **Add tusks.** Cut two 8" (20 cm) pieces of white yarn. Insert the white yarn at each bobble's base and go down two rows. Tie knots to secure the yarn, then tuck the knot and excess yarn inside the walrus. Pull on each of the white pieces to make sure they are sufficiently visible.

***Finished Size:***
10" × 6" (25 × 15 cm)

***Skill Level:***
Confident Beginner
(Intermediate if making a gray snout)

*Whale Variation:*

# SEAL

Sheila the Seal has a whiskery mustache and pink cheeks to make her distinct. The love really is in the details!

If you need extra guidance while making any of the standard parts of this project, refer to the more detailed instructions for Whale on page 102!

## SUPPLIES

**Chunky blanket yarn:**
White: 15 yards (13.7 m)
Black: 1 foot (30 cm)
Gray (optional): 1 yard
Pink (optional): 1 foot (30 cm)

**Fiberfill: 2 ounces (55 g)**

**Scissors**

All finished sizes, yarn lengths, and fiberfill quantities are approximate.

## BODY

1 **Start the body.** With white yarn, create a slip knot that has an 8" (20 cm) tail. Make the slip-knot loop about 1½" (3.8 cm) or two fingers wide. Chain on a total of 10 loops for Row 1. Make the chain row (Row 1) into a circle by pulling the tail yarn through loop 10 of the chain row. Then knit standard rows as follows: Rows 2–3: Knit 10 (20 loops total).

2 **Start Row 4.** Row 4 includes a color change, a bobble (see page 95 for instructions), and a reverse bobble (see page 118 for instructions). The entire rows is as follows: Row 4: Knit 3, bobble 1, reverse bobble 1, knit 5. Let's walk through the details. First, knit 3, then attach the gray yarn to the last loop with a knot—but don't cut the white off.

3 **Make the normal bobble.** With the gray yarn, make a bobble, but instead of pulling the last loop of the bobble up with the gray, finish the bobble with the white yarn (bring the white yarn from the inside of the project over to the right side of the bobble and pull up the loop from the right to the left).

4 **Make the reverse bobble.** Do the same with the reverse bobble: Keep the white yarn on the left side of the bobble and pull up the loop from the left to the right. You should knit the first 2 loops of the bobble with the gray yarn, and then decrease with the white yarn.

**5** **Finish the gray yarn.** Cut the gray yarn, leaving 4" (10 cm), and tie a knot on the white yarn to secure it in place. Pick up with the white yarn to continue the row: knit 5.

**6** **Check your work and finish the body.** Here is your finished seal snout! After this, complete the body by knitting standard rows as follows: Rows 5–10: Knit 10 (60 loops total).

## TAIL

**7** **Make the tail.** Refer to steps 5–12 of Whale (page 105) for how to make the tail—the only difference is that you're using white yarn and that when you weave the excess yarn down the right side of the chain, weave until it is one row up from the tail yarn.

**8** **Attach the tail.** Refer to steps 13–15 of Whale (page 107) for how to attach the tail—the only difference is that you should place the tail horizontally in between a column (the column the tail yarn is lined up with), three rows up from the bottom.

## FINS (×2)

**9** **Make and add the fins.** Refer to steps 16–17 of Whale (page 107) for how to make and attach the fins—the only difference is that you're using white yarn and that the placement is slightly different: Place the fins on the third row up from the bottom, in line with the tail.

## NOSE

**10** **Add the nose.** Cut an 8" (20 cm) piece of black yarn and wrap it twice around the center row, right above the 2 bobbles, to create the nose. On each side of the nose, put the strands on the inside of the seal and tie a double knot to secure the nose in place.

## EYES (×2) AND FINISHING

**11** **Add eyes and close up.** Cut two 6" (16 cm) pieces of black yarn and tie a single knot at the center of each piece. Insert the eyes one column over from the fins (one column to the side and above the bobbles). Secure them with a double knot on the inside of the body. For the blush, cut two 6" (16 cm) pieces of pink yarn and insert them one row below the eyes and through just one loop on the outer side of each eye, then tie them off on the inside as well. Close the bottom of the seal, following the standard instructions (work to the right, pulling from the outside to the inside). Stuff the seal with fiberfill. Then close the top of the seal, following the standard instructions (work to the left, pulling from the inside to the outside).

***Finished Size:***
12" × 9" (31 × 23 cm)

***Skill Level:***
Intermediate

# ELEPHANT

Ellie the Elephant and Penelope the Pig have been with me since I started my stuffie design journey. As my finger-knitting skills have evolved, these patterns have undergone countless updates and refinements. Finalizing a pattern is one of the most rewarding parts of being a pattern designer; it's that moment when everything feels just right. Sometimes the process is quick, but other times, it takes months or even years of adjustments and building confidence before sharing something with the world. Ellie the Elephant and Penelope the Pig required months of dedication and fine-tuning. I'm excited to share these two special patterns, knowing they've reached their best versions. They are the perfect conclusion to this book, offering an engaging challenge for intermediate-level crafters.

## SUPPLIES

**Chunky blanket yarn:**
Light gray: 29 yards (26.5 m)
Black: 1 foot (30 cm)

**Fiberfill: 6 ounces (170 g)**

**Scissors**

All finished sizes, yarn lengths, and fiberfill quantities are approximate.

## BODY

1 **Make the body.** With the light-gray yarn, create a slip knot that has an 8" (20 cm) tail. Make the slip-knot loop about 1½" (3.8 cm) or two fingers wide. Chain on a total of 12 loops for Row 1. Make the chain row (Row 1) into a circle by pulling the tail yarn through loop 12 of the chain row. Then knit standard rows as follows: Row 2–17: Knit 12 (192 loops total). Cut the working yarn off the skein, leaving a tail of about 8" (20 cm).

## FEET (×4)

2 **Start the foot.** Grab your skein of light-gray yarn again. About five rows down from the top of the body, going from the inside, push up 4 loops in a square around a single body row. This will be considered Row 1 of this foot. Make sure to leave an 8" (20 cm) tail of yarn on the inside.

3 **Cut and secure the foot.** Cut the working yarn to a length of 1½ feet (45 cm), then tie a double knot with the tail yarn and working yarn on the inside of the body. Don't pull the knot too hard—you want the loops to stay in place, not slip out!

4 **Knit the next foot row.** Pull the working yarn to the outside of the body, through the middle of the foot loops, leaving the tail yarn on the inside. Then knit standard row as follows: Row 2: Knit 4.

**5 Close off the foot.** Close the loops of the foot by pulling the yarn through each loop, going from the inside toward the outside. Don't close it too tight, though—you'll need enough space to pull the yarn through the center of the hole in the next step.

**6 Secure the finished foot.** Bring the excess working yarn through the center of the foot hole you just closed up and to the inside of the body. Tie a double knot with the tail yarn and working yarn again to secure everything in place.

**7 Make the other feet.** Make three more feet, following the same steps. Place one foot one half column over from the first foot and place the other pair of feet a few rows down, in line with the first pair.

**8 Close the front.** Close the front of the elephant's body (the end where the open loops are and where you cut the working yarn at the end of step 1). Pull the working yarn through each loop from the inside of the project toward the outside, working to the left. Once finished, make a double knot at the base of the working yarn and then push the working yarn and knot through the center of the hole.

## EARS (×2)

**9 Start the ear.** Grab your skein of light-gray yarn again; we're going to start Row 1 of the right ear. With the bottom of the elephant facing away from you, leave an 8" (20 cm) tail of yarn and pull up 4 loops leading vertically away from the right front foot, starting one column above the foot. I have my finger through the starting spot here, ready to pull up the first of the 4 loops.

**10 Continue Row 1 of the ear.** And here I've pulled up the first of the 4 loops of Row 1 of the ear. Continue vertically (that is, away from the foot) to pull up the other 3 loops.

**11 Finish knitting the ear.** Continue knitting the ear with two more rows as follows. Row 2: Going back in the opposite direction (toward the foot), knit 4. Row 3: Going in the opposite direction again (away from the foot), knit 1, increase, knit 2, increase, knit 1 (6 loops total).

**12 Close off the ear.** Knit a final closing row to close off the 6 loops. That is, pull up 2 loops, take the first loop made, and pull it over the top of and down around the second loop made, etc. When you have 1 loop left, cut the working yarn to 8" (20 cm), pull it through the last loop, and tighten it to close it off. Weave the excess yarn down the ear and to the bottom.

**13** **Secure the ear.** Pull the tail yarn to the inside of the elephant's body, then pull it back out one row over—still on the backside of the ear, and one column away from the excess working yarn you cut off in 12. Tie a double knot with the two strands of yarn, then push the knot and yarn strands to the inside of the body.

**14** **Make the other ear.** Now make an elephant ear on the left side, following the same steps. Make sure the ears line up from the top of the elephant.

## NOSE

**15** **Start the nose.** Make a slip knot and chain on a total of 8 loops. Count down one side of the chain and pull up another loop three loops down on the side of the chain. Pull the second-to-last loop made (loop 8 of the chain) over the top of and down around the side loop you just made. From here, repeat to continue pulling up 1 new side loop and then closing it off with the previous loop all the way down the same side, until there is just 1 loop left. Close this last loop off by pulling the excess yarn through it.

**16** **Even out the strands.** Take the tail yarn and wrap it around the final loop right above it until the two strands are matching lengths.

17 **Insert the nose.** Insert the two nose strands at the front of the face (toward the bottom) and right at the middle of the two front feet. Go inside the elephant and tie a single knot with the two strands, then bring one of the strands to the top of the face, and push it to the outside, just to the right or left of the center.

18 **Secure the nose.** Push the strand through a loop on the elephant's nose, then bring the strand back to the inside of the elephant, on the opposite side. Secure the nose by tying a double knot on the inside of the body with the two nose strands.

## EYES (×2) AND FINISHING

19 **Make and add the eyes.** Cut two 6" (16 cm) pieces of black yarn and tie a single knot at the center of each piece. Insert each eye at the front of the elephant, with a single knot on the inside and the two strands on the outside. Once the eyes are in place, tie a double knot with each strand. Then flip the double knots to the inside of the elephant and push the single knot to the outside of the elephant.

**20** **Stuff and close.** Stuff the elephant with fiberfill. Pull the tail yarn through each bottom loop from the outside toward the inside, working to the right and tightening gently as you go. Once finished, make a double knot at the base of the tail yarn and then push the tail yarn and knot through the center of the hole.

**21** **Make the tail.** Bring the excess strand of tail yarn back outside the body, right above the circle's center, to serve as the tail.

***Finished Size:***
12" × 9" (31 × 23 cm)

***Skill Level:***
Intermediate

# PIG

I can still picture the first photo I ever shared of Penelope the Pig on my Instagram stories. It was just an unfinished prototype, with no eyes and not even stuffed yet, but I was so excited to be working on my third-ever stuffie that I couldn't wait to post it, even with my tiny following. I honestly had no idea what I was doing, but I was thrilled that it kind of looked like a pig. Like Ellie the Elephant, Penelope has gone through a lot of fine-tuning over the years. It's taken time, trial and error, and growing confidence to get her pattern to the point where I finally feel ready to share it.

## SUPPLIES

**Chunky blanket yarn:**
Light pink: 25 yards (22.9 m)
Dark pink: 2 yards (1.8 m)
Black: 1 foot (30 cm)

**Fiberfill: 6 ounces (170 g)**

**Scissors**

All finished sizes, yarn lengths, and fiberfill quantities are approximate.

## BODY AND FEET

**1 Make the body and add feet.** With light-pink yarn, follow steps 1–8 of Elephant (page 130) to create the body, add four feet, and close up the front.

## SNOUT

**2 Start the snout.** With dark-pink yarn, at the front of the pig's body, pull up 6 loops in a circle around the center of the hole that you just closed up. This will be Row 1 of the snout. Make sure to leave an 8" (20 cm) tail of yarn.

**3 Knit a second snout row.** Tie a double knot with the tail yarn and working yarn. Push the tail yarn and knot to the inside of the pig's body. With the working yarn, knit a standard row as follows: Row 2: Knit 6.

**4 Finish the snout.** Cut the working yarn, leaving about an 8" (20 cm) tail, and close the snout. (Closing the snout is just like closing the foot as explained in the Elephant: working to the left and from the inside toward the outside.) Insert the excess yarn through the center of the hole to the inside of the pig's body. Inside the body, tie a double knot with the two strands of yarn from the snout, securing it to the front of the body.

**5 Stuff and close up.** Stuff the pig with fiberfill. Then close up the bottom of the pig: Pull the tail yarn through each bottom loop from the outside toward the inside, working to the right and tightening gently as you go. Once finished, make a double knot at the base of the tail yarn and then push the tail yarn and knot through the center of the hole. To make the tail, bring the excess strand of yarn back out just above the circle's center.

## EARS (×2)

**6 Start one ear.** With light-pink yarn and with the bottom of the pig facing away from you, pull up 2 loops at the top left of the pig's body, going horizontally (parallel to the pig's face). (With the front of the pig facing toward you, this will be the left side for you, but technically the pig's right ear). This is Row 1 of this ear. Leave an 8" (20 cm) tail of yarn. Then knit a standard row as follows: Row 2: Knit 2.

**7 Finish the ear.** Continue this ear by knitting the next row as follow: Row 3: Knit 1, decrease. After completing this row, close the last loop by cutting the working yarn, leaving about an 8" (20 cm) tail, then gently pulling the yarn through the previous loop and tightening it. Weave the yarn down on the left side and tie a double knot with the tail yarn. Push the knot and excess yarn to the inside of the pig.

8 **Make the other ear.** Grab your skein of light-pink yarn again. With the bottom of the pig facing away from you, pull up 2 loops at the top right of the pig's body, going horizontally (parallel to the pig's face). (With the front of the pig facing toward you, this will be the right side for you, but technically the pig's left ear). This is Row 1 of this ear. Knit Rows 2–3 (4 loops total) and finish this ear the same way as you did for the first ear (see steps 6–7).

## EYES (×2)

9 **Add eyes and close up.** Cut two 6" (16 cm) pieces of black yarn and tie a single knot at the center of each piece. Insert each eye at the front of the pig, with a single knot on the inside and the two strands on the outside. Once you have the eyes in place, tie a double knot with each strand, flip the double knots to the inside of the pig, and push the single knot to the outside of the pig.

# MORE FINGER-KNITTING FUN!

*If you loved this book, be sure to check out the Jiggle the Jellyfish and Sugarplum Christmas Tree kits!*

Perfect for beginners and beyond, each kit includes everything you need to craft your creation: soft, chunky yarn in all the colors required, soft fiberfill for shaping your creation, a 16-page instructional booklet with clear step-by-step guidance, exclusive access to an online video tutorial led by the author, and even an adorable sticker to collect as you work through the series.

Enjoy the fun of finger knitting or give it as a gift to someone special!

**Super Simple Finger Knitting Kit Jiggle the Jellyfish**
ISBN 978-0-7643-7044-1 | $29.99

**Super Simple Finger Knitting Kit Sugarplum Christmas Tree**
ISBN 978-0-7643-7043-4 | $29.99

# INDEX

**Note: Page numbers in *italics* indicate projects.**